For Christ and his church

FOR CHRIST AND HIS CHURCH

Essays in service of the church and its mission

Contributors
Rick Reed
Michael Haykin
Barry Howson
David Barker
Wayne Baxter
Gord Oeste
Cyril Guérette
Marianne Vanderboom
Stan Fowler

joshua
press

press

www.joshuapress.com

Published by
Joshua Press Inc., Kitchener, Ontario, Canada
Distributed by
Sola Scriptura Ministries International
www.sola-scriptura.ca

Cover and book design by Janice Van Eck

Library and Archives Canada Cataloguing in Publication

    For Christ and his church : essays in service of the church and its mission / contributors, Rick Reed [and eight others].

ISBN 978-1-894400-65-7 (pbk.)

    1. Pastoral theology—Baptists. I. Reed, Rick, 1957–, author

BV4011.3.F67 2015   253   C2015-900894-8

Dedicated to the past and present students, faculty and alumni of Heritage College & Seminary

Contents

Contributors

FROM THE FACULTY OF HERITAGE COLLEGE & SEMINARY, CAMBRIDGE, ONTARIO, CANADA

Rick Reed, President, Professor of Homiletics and Pastoral Studies
Michael Haykin, Professor of Church History
Barry Howson, Academic Dean (College), Director of Religious Studies
David Barker, Vice President—Academics and Student Affairs,
    Academic Dean (Seminary)
Wayne Baxter, Professor of New Testament
Gord Oeste, Professor of Old Testament
Cyril Guérette, Professor of Theology and Philosophy
Marianne Vanderboom, Assistant to the Dean (College),
    Director of Bachelor of Religious Education Professional
Stan Fowler, Professor of Theological Studies

Preface

BY RICK REED

"What makes your school effective?"

That's the question a Christian journalist asked me to answer for a feature she was doing on seminaries. Her question was both fair and important. It was also a question that raised other questions: Are we actually effective as a school? How do we gauge effectiveness?

My response to this journalist's question was that we gauge our effectiveness as a school by how valuable we are to the church. I responded that way because Heritage College & Seminary exists for Christ and his church.

At Heritage, we understand the church is central to God's redemptive plan. Our role as a school is to help the church to fulfil its mission in the world. Our faculty see themselves as "scholars in service of the church"—to use Dr. Fowler's phrase. We seek to support, strengthen and sharpen the church by assisting its leaders (both present and future) to become more biblically solid and spiritually vibrant.

This book is part of our effort to serve the church. In the chapters that follow, you will find a collection of articles written by faculty members at Heritage College & Seminary. Each professor seeks to leverage his or her learning for the good of Christ's church, applying academic study to ministry situations.

How will we know if this book is effective? We'll gauge that by whether or not it helps people like you become more effective in serving Christ, his church and its mission.

For Christ and his church,

Rick Reed, President, and the Faculty at Heritage College & Seminary, Cambridge, Ontario, Canada

01

Mending a broken engagement: Reuniting God's people with God's Word

BY RICK REED

vangelicals are Bible people. We believe the Bible is God's Word. We preach the Bible in our churches. We read the Bible in our homes.

At least we used to.

If you examine the results of a recent study conducted by the Evangelical Fellowship of Canada, you will see evidence that things are changing, and not for the better.

In 2013, the Evangelical Fellowship of Canada released the results of the Canadian Bible Engagement Study (www.bibleengagement-study.ca). This study sought to quantify the percentage of Canadians who engage meaningfully with the Bible by reading it, reflecting on it and discussing it with others. The report shows that trends in

Canada are moving strongly toward greater disengagement with the Bible rather than greater engagement with it:

The percentage of frequent Bible readers has dropped significantly in the last two decades, for the general population and for Christians. In 1996, 21% of Canadians reported reading the Bible at least weekly, compared to 11% in 2013. Among Christians, the percentage of those who read at least weekly fell from 27% in 1996 to 14% in 2013.[1]

Not only has the percentage of Christians who read the Bible weekly tumbled by half in the past two decades, a large number of evangelicals (36%) now admit to reading the Bible "seldom" or "never."[2] In short, more and more Canadian Christians are reading the Bible less and less.

Christians who have a deficient diet of God's Word inevitably become anaemic and malnourished. They lack the vitality they need to stay spiritually healthy. They lose the energy they need to sustain a robust ministry.

I remember my dad telling the congregation he pastored, "Seven days without the Bible makes one weak." As a kid, I thought that saying was pretty amusing. Now I see it as painfully accurate.

How did we get here?

While there are undoubtedly a number of reasons why Christians are increasingly disengaged from Scripture, the Canadian Bible Engagement Study highlights one of the major causes: loss of confidence in the Bible.

Confidence in the Bible has taken a big hit in the past two decades. The number of Canadians who are convinced the Bible is the Word of God has declined from 35% in 1996 to 18% in 2013.[3] Seven out of ten Canadians (and one in four evangelicals) believe the Bible has "irreconcilable contradictions."[4]

---

1 Hiemstra, Rick, ed., *Confidence, Conversation and Community: Bible Engagement in Canada, 2013* (Toronto: Faith Today Publications, 2014), 9.
2 Hiemstra, *Bible Engagement in Canada*, 10.
3 Hiemstra, *Bible Engagement in Canada*, 5.
4 Hiemstra, *Bible Engagement in Canada*, 16.

When confidence in the Bible dips—even a bit—engagement with the Bible plummets. Among evangelicals who "strongly agree that the Bible is God's Word," 61% read it at least several times a week. By contrast, only 3% of evangelicals who "moderately agree the Bible is God's Word" read it more than once a week.[5]

Stop for a moment and let that sink in: 61% of Christians who have "strong" confidence in the Bible read it more than once a week. But only 3% of those who have "moderate" confidence in the Bible read it at least weekly:

> Canadians who frequently read the Bible are confident that it is the reliable word of God, with a message that is unique among world religions and relevant to their lives. Those who strongly agree that the Bible is the Word of God are far more likely to read and reflect on it and attend religious services than those who only moderately agree.[6]

While there has always been an assault on the reliability of the Bible, we live in a day when the attack has become high profile and widespread. Not only is this attack coming from skeptical professors at secular universities, it is coming from some who claim Christian loyalties. For example, a theologian who teaches at a Christian university recently published a book that contends the Bible is riddled with internal contradictions and historical inaccuracies. In spite of this, he still believes we should read the Bible for spiritual benefit.

If this professor would read the results of the Canadian Bible Engagement Study, he would be hit with a harsh truth. His viewpoint, which undermines confidence in the Bible's reliability, has a drastic impact on the Bible's readability. The subtitle on his book's cover says, "Why defending Scripture has made us unable to read it." Actually, the sobering truth is that undermining confidence in Scripture makes us unwilling to read it.

---

5 Hiemstra, *Bible Engagement in Canada*, 15.
6 Hiemstra, *Bible Engagement in Canada*, 12.

Time to turn it around

Having highlighted the downward trend toward greater *disengagement* with the Bible, it's time to consider what can be done to turn things around. Like all spiritual transformations, a change for the better will ultimately be a work of God's Spirit. But God's Spirit often works through God's people to accomplish his will.

There are a number of ways pastors and other church leaders can cooperate with God's Spirit to encourage a greater engagement with God's Word. I'll highlight four ways that hold great promise for help.

1. Model engagement with the Bible

"You cannot impart what you do not possess." That's a saying I heard repeatedly from Dr. Howard Hendricks during my seminary days. He was reminding us that our pastoral impact is linked to our personal example.

Increasing Bible engagement in our congregations begins by modeling it in our own lives. In our hallway conversations, counselling appointments, board meetings, prayers and sermons, it should be apparent that we are personally and presently engaged with the Bible—reading it, meditating on it, rejoicing in it and responding to it. It should be obvious that we echo David's delight in Scripture: "How I love your law. I meditate on it all day long" (Psalm 119:97). It must be clear that we are seeking to align our personal convictions and ministry decisions with the teaching of God's Word.

A pastoral example of this kind of deep engagement with Scripture is John Bunyan, the author of *Pilgrim's Progress*. Charles Spurgeon had this to say about Bunyan: "Why, this man is a living Bible! Prick him anywhere; his blood is Bibline, the very essence of the Bible flows from him. He cannot speak without quoting a text, for his very soul is full of the Word of God."[7]

Here's a question we must ask ourselves: Would the people who know me best say my "very soul is full of the Word of God"? If we

---

[7] Quoted by Justin Taylor, "Do You Bleed Bibline?" Gospel Coalition Blog (http://www. thegospelcoalition.org/blogs/justintaylor/2011/08/11/do-you-bleed-bibline/; accessed December 19, 2014).

hope to call others to engage with Scripture, it must be evident that we are enthusiastically leading the way. To quote another one of Dr. Hendricks's favourite sayings, "If you want them to bleed, you have to hemorrhage."

2. Preach through the text to the heart

We need to preach expositional sermons. While there are different definitions of expository preaching, from my perspective an excellent expository sermon is one that travels through the text to the heart.

Expositors don't treat a passage of Scripture as a runway at Pearson International Airport; they don't simply take off from it and quickly leave it behind. Rather, they see their preaching text as a hiking trail in Algonquin Park; expositors lead people on a journey through a passage. They follow the terrain of the text in order to "expose" the biblical author's main message.

This journey through the text has a definite destination—it heads toward the heart. Excellent expositors aren't satisfied to simply dispense biblical truth. They seek, in reliance on the Holy Spirit, to give information that leads to inspiration and transformation. Expository preachers are faithful to the original meaning of the text but never forget that the ultimate objective of Scripture is to bring people into a life-changing relationship with God through Christ.

You may be wondering what this call for expository preaching has to do with increasing Bible engagement in the congregation. My answer is simple: Bible exposition from the pastor encourages Bible engagement in the congregation. Expository preaching, because of its close adherence to the biblical text, demonstrates a strong confidence in the authority of Scripture. Preachers who base their words on God's Word and bend their thoughts to his truth give their congregations an indirect apologetic for the authority of the Bible. And remember, the Bible Engagement Study revealed that only those with "strong confidence" in Scripture read it regularly.

Furthermore, exposition shows individuals in the congregation how to approach Scripture—first you seek to understand the original message of the text, and then you discern its contemporary application. In other words, expository preaching models a method of Bible reading and study that Christians can utilize throughout the week.

3. Become an open Bible church on Sundays

In my role as president at Heritage College & Seminary, I often travel to speak at different churches on Sunday mornings. One disheartening trend I've noticed is that very few people seem to be looking at their own copy of the Scriptures (printed or electronic) while I'm preaching.

In some cases, the reason for the lack of open Bibles is that we've unintentionally discipled people *not* to bring a Bible to church. We've trained people not to bring a Bible to church by displaying the sermon passage on the screen. Why open a Bible when it's projected on the big screen? We've also taught people Bibles are optional by preaching sermons that are only marginally tied to Scripture. Why open a Bible when it's not being examined or exposited?

Retraining our people to bring and open their Bibles at church will take some intentionality. Here are several ways pastors can work to develop an "open Bible" culture in their congregations.

First, be wise in the Scripture you choose to project on the screens or print in the bulletin. Do project the verses you select for the public reading of Scripture—a necessity in this day of multiple translations. Don't put the main Scripture text for the sermon on the big screen. Instead, display only the additional supportive verses that are mentioned during the message.

Second, make Bibles available to those who don't have one when they arrive at church. Encourage people to open to the passage for the message by telling them the page number in the Bibles you've provided. This will help the uninitiated find the passage without feeling foolish and will emphasize your desire to have Bibles open during the message.

Third, repeatedly refer to the text of Scripture during your sermon. Say, "Look with me again at what it says in verse 16," or "Did you notice the phrase Paul uses in verse 5?" Keep pointing people to the text to highlight that open Bibles are essential to getting the most out of the message. John Piper's advice to young preachers needs to be heard by all preachers:

My continual advice to beginning preachers is, "Quote the text! Quote the text! Say the actual words of the text again and again. Show the people where your ideas are coming from." Most people do not easily follow the connections a preacher sees between his words and the text. They must be shown again and again with actual quotes from Scripture.[8]

If we want people to open their Bibles at home during the week, we can start by getting them to open them at church on Sundays.

4. Become an open Bible church all week long
While we want to get people engaging with Scripture on Sundays, our goal is far greater. We hope to see Scripture shape lives all week long. One of the ways to encourage this is to get people talking about the Bible during the week.

The Canadian Bible Engagement Study found that those who reflect on the meaning of Scripture and discuss it with others are the most engaged with the Bible. "Our study found that reflection on the meaning of the Bible for people's lives is an important kind of Bible engagement, but that conversation with others about the meaning of the Bible is the key factor in deepening Bible engagement."[9]

How can we encourage and increase this kind of Bible engagement during the week? Here are several ways.

First, churches can provide study guides for the pastor's upcoming sermon series. These study guides function like seasoned trail guides—they draw attention to important features in the text and promote personal discovery of biblical truth. The study guides can also contain discussion questions for the passage that can be used by families or small groups.

When I served as a pastor at the Metropolitan Bible Church in Ottawa, we produced study and discussion guides for some of our upcoming sermon series (normally the fall series). While the time and effort required to prepare these study guides was consider-

---

8 John Piper, *The Supremacy of God in Preaching* (Grand Rapids: Baker Book House, 2004), 86.
9 Hiemstra, *Bible Engagement in Canada*, 6.

able, so was the increase of congregational engagement in studying and discussing of Scripture.

Second, make sure your small groups are big on Bible engagement. Many churches have small groups that meet to discuss how Sunday's sermon can be lived out during the week. In order to maximize biblical engagement, discussion questions should prompt group members to open their Bibles, review the sermon passage and then base their responses on the explicit teaching of the Bible. Group leaders should be trained to help group members link their applicational responses to Scriptural truth.

A movement of biblically engaged churches

Years ago I was given a poster with these words: "He who has books but doesn't read them is no better off than the one who cannot read." While this saying has merit for books in general, it's especially true for someone who has a Bible but doesn't read it.

Canada is a country that has a nearly prefect literacy rate (99%). While we've almost eliminated illiteracy in Canada, our biblical illiteracy rate is growing at an alarming rate. If this trend continues we will see more congregations made up of people who are functionally illiterate when it comes to God's Word.

There is an urgent need for churches to help reverse this trend. These churches will be led by pastors who understand that Bible engagement is foundational to the spiritual life of individual Christians as well as the entire congregation.

These pastors and church leaders will intentionally and relentlessly focus effort and energy on getting believers to get into God's Word. They will model personal engagement with Scripture. They will seek to motivate others to read Scripture, reflect on it, discuss it with others and submit to its teaching. They will take personally a statement Dietrich Bonhoeffer once made to a group of aspiring pastors: "The best sign of a good pastor is that the congregation reads the Bible."[10]

---

10 Dietrich Bonhoeffer, *Theological Education at Finkenwalde: 1935–1937*. Vol. 14. Dietrich Bonhoeffer, *Works*, ed. H. Gaylon Barker and Mark Brocker (Minneapolis: Fortress Press, 2013), 489.

02

"We desire a learned ministry...we desire a pious ministry": Remembering the vision of Benjamin Davies for Canada Baptist College

BY MICHAEL HAYKIN

t has been one of the greatest privileges of my life to serve the evangelical Baptist churches of Ontario through the medium of theological education. Like other areas of vocational ministry, it has not been without its challenges, one of which has been the lackadaisical attitude toward formal theological education on the part of far too many Baptist congregations in the province. Historically, though, this attitude has deep roots in Ontario Baptist soil. While Methodists and Presbyterians in what would become Ontario recognized the importance of having a theological college early on, it would not be until 1860, nearly eighty years after Baptists had first come into Ontario that they would have a successful school for training pastors, what was known as the Canadian Literary Institute, in Woodstock.

Canada Baptist College

There had been an earlier attempt to fund such a school, Canada Baptist College, in Montreal, but it had failed in 1849 after only eleven years of operation. This school had its origins in the earliest days of the Ottawa Association, when, in 1836, it recommended that an academy be established in either Upper or Lower Canada to train men for the Baptist ministry.[1] That very year, John Gilmour (1792–1869), a Scottish Baptist who was the pastor of First Baptist Church, Montreal, sailed to England to seek to raise support for a possible seminary. His trip was not in vain, for Gilmour returned in March 1837, with between £1500–£1600 (probably close to $880,000 in today's currency) for an educational institution.[2]

A number of sites for the new college were considered. Eventually a site in Montreal was chosen, possibly because it was the centre of British banking and business interests. Thus, on September 24, 1838, Canada Baptist College opened its doors in Montreal with two students.[3] The school curriculum was curious in some ways. For instance, along with the biblical languages, Hebrew and Greek, the students were also taught Latin, Syriac and German, but not French, even though the school was situated in Montreal!

Its first principal was Benjamin Davies (1814–1875), a Welsh Baptist scholar, who had secured a Ph.D. from the University of Leipzig in 1838 when he was only twenty-four. The first Ph.D. in a Canadian institution of higher learning, he directed the school from 1838 to 1843.[4] During his five years at the school, roughly thirty students benefited from his teaching and counsel.[5] In a circular letter that Davies drew up for the Ottawa Association in 1840,

---

1 A.H. Newman, "Sketch of the Baptists of Ontario and Quebec to 1851," *The Baptist Year Book* (Historical Number) (1900), 80.
2 Newman, "Sketch of the Baptists," 81–82.
3 For the story of the school, see George W. Campbell, "Canada Baptist College, 1838–1849. The Generation and Demise of a Pioneering Dream in Canadian Theological Education" (M.Th. thesis, Knox College, University of Toronto, 1974).
4 On Davies, see J.H.Y. Briggs, "Davies, Benjamin." In *The Blackwell Dictionary of Evangelical Biography 1730–1860*. Vol. 1, ed. Donald M. Lewis (Oxford/Cambridge: Blackwell Publishers, 1995), 295.
5 *Montreal Register*, 3 (February 22, 1844), 2.

the Baptist educator provides a concise overview of his view of theological education. It is an overview that is still instructive— would that Ontario Baptists had always heeded its wisdom over the past 175 years!

A perspective on theological education

Deep distrust of theological education has long been endemic among Baptists. In the mid-eighteenth century, for example, the deacons of the Baptist cause in Westbury Leigh, Wiltshire, England, regarded

> Human learning in a pastor with feelings of suspicion, and entertained the strongest aversion to those whom they termed "men-made" ministers....The Bristol Academy.. presented the nearest object of mistrust to the members at Westbury Leigh....They could never bring themselves to regard this seat of human learning with any degree of complacency; and they scorned, as they said, "to go down to Egypt for help."[6]

A similar attitude was discernible among Ontario Baptist in the mid-nineteenth century. As Davies wrote, "it is to be feared there are some, who look upon it [i.e. theological education] with jealousy, if not with hostility."[7]

Seeking to disarm this hostility, Davies pointed out, on the one hand, that the support of formal theological education in no way entailed the belief that "none can be worthy and useful ministers without education." In fact, there were a good number of examples to the contrary in the history of the church. The early apostles were an eminent example in this regard. Nevertheless, Davies argued, the reason why such uneducated individuals succeed is either because they labour among "people as uncultivated as themselves" or they possess "natural powers of mind." Illustrative of the latter was John Bunyan (1628–1688), who, though an

---

6 John Clark Marshman, *The Life and Times of Carey, Marshman and Ward* (London: Longman, Brown, Green, Longmans, & Roberts, 1859), 1:105–106.

7 "Ministerial Education," *The Canada Baptist Magazine*, 3, no.9 (March 1840): 193.

"untutored tinker," had a natural genius which made of him "a mighty preacher and an immortal author." In fact, Davies was quick to point out, there were many uneducated ministers who "are often heard lamenting their deficiencies, and coveting learning as a help to them in their work." Davies saw a good example in this regard in another English Baptist, Andrew Fuller (1754–1815),

> of blessed memory, who began to preach when very unlearned, but who was so sensible of his disadvantages that he used great diligence to acquire that knowledge, without which he could never be, what he at length became, one of the most valuable men of his time, and decidedly the most useful minister in our religious community.[8]

On the other hand, not for a moment did Davies believe that "education alone, apart from moral adaptation, can qualify for the ministry."[9] Responding to those who were coming to regard ministerial training in the same terms as training for any other profession, Davies vehemently asserted:

> It is a notorious fact, that in all secular or state churches, young men are raised to undertake 'the care of souls,' without any regard to their religious feelings. We however utterly reprobate such a notion and such a custom. Much as we desire a *learned* ministry, we desire a *pious* ministry more. The first and most essential qualification, which we look for and demand, is godliness, while we seek learning only as a secondary, though not unimportant preparation. It is our solemn conviction that no literary attainments, no powers of rhetoric, can give fitness for the work, if the heart be not engaged in it. This preparation of the heart in man must come from the Lord, before any other preparation, whether of erudition or of eloquence, can qualify him for the ministry.[10]

---

8 "Ministerial Education," 194–195.
9 "Ministerial Education," 195.
10 "Ministerial Education," 195–196.

In training a man for pastoral ministry, learning, though important, is not as vital as piety. It is the latter—the engagement of the
heart, the longing for holiness, the love of human beings—which
is absolutely indispensable in a pastor's life. And this piety is itself
God's creation. In other words, unlike other professions, genuine
pastoral ministry must arise from a calling from God.

The necessity of a college

In seeking to raise support for Canada Baptist College, a place of
formal study, Davies had no intention of casting aspersions on
other, more informal methods of education. "If the learning itself
be sound and to the purpose," he rightly noted, "we care not
much whether it has been gained at home, or in the collegiate
seats of liberal education, or in the halls of divinity." Davies could
point to a number of self-taught men in the transatlantic Baptist
community which amply demonstrated his point:

> Who does not know the history of our illustrious [William]
> Carey, how he became a prodigy of learning, without having
> ever frequented the groves of Academus? How happy a cir-
> cumstance would it be for the cause of truth, if unlettered
> ministers generally were to follow the bright example of
> Carey, Fuller, [Abraham] Booth and others, by struggling
> through their difficulties and placing themselves on a level
> with the well instructed and enlightened![11]

But Davies was a realist and knew that the achievements of a Wil-
liam Carey or an Andrew Fuller were probably too much to expect
of most men. A theological college was thus a necessity.

Among the goals of such an institution, Davies noted two in
particular. First, a formal theological education will "greatly assist"
budding pastors "in studying and understanding the Scriptures."
Without a doubt, what the Bible has to say about "the way of
salvation and the principal duties incumbent on man" is easy to
understand. Yet, even the apostle Peter had to admit that in Paul's
writings there are "some things hard to be understood, which they

---

11 "Ministerial Education," 196.

that are unlearned and unstable wrest, as they do also the other scriptures, unto their own destruction" [2 Peter 3:16, KJV].

A close reading of the Scriptures reveals other areas of difficulty. As Davies noted, though, this should not be considered surprising.

> A collection of writings, that are of such high antiquity, several of them being the most ancient in existence, that were composed by Orientals for the use, in the first place, of people, whose mode of living, thinking, and speaking differed widely from our own, that treat on the most sublime and abstruse subjects, and that too in languages which have long since ceased to be spoken, and therefore not easily mastered, and that have been handed down for many generations by the labour of the pen, which is a process far less favourable to correctness than printing—surely a collection of such a character, must be expected to contain parts, exceedingly obscure to us, however clear they may have been to the first readers.[12]

Understanding the cultural, intellectual, and linguistic differences between the world in which the Bible was written and nineteenth-century British North America, as well as having some cognizance of the various difficulties posed by the transmission of the biblical text, required theological education if the text was to be faithfully proclaimed to Canadians. Nor can a preacher simply trust commentaries to relieve him of his difficulties. If he does, he is at the mercy of those who write them. "Every professed and public expounder of the lively oracles," Davies averred, should "desire and...be able to form an enlightened and matured opinion" of the texts on which he is speaking. Davies pointed out that this would obviously entail some understanding of the original languages, a further reason for formal training.[13]

A second major reason why education was needed was to enable ministers to be more effective in their explanation of God's Word to others. A good theological training helps those who are to be ministers to present their beliefs intelligibly, cogently and in a

---

12 "Ministerial Education," 197.
13 "Ministerial Education," 197–198.

winsome fashion. It enables them to order their sermons so that they do "not present a confused mass of ideas, jumbled together without connection and without design." Davies was well aware that the age in which he lived was one in which various "learned criticisms" were being advanced against the truths of the Scriptures. How could the Bible be defended, though, without some education?[14]

Davies closed with a fervent appeal.

> Having thus, beloved brethren, laid before you the subject of ministerial education, we cannot close without affectionately urging you to support the theological institution [Canada Baptist College] now established among us. Will you permit it to decline and fall, by withholding from it your prayers and contributions? Will those who have the means to provide education for pious and gifted young men, who thirst for improvement, deny them any assistance? Unfaithfulness in this matter must be positive treachery to the cause.[15]

By and large, though, Davies' appeal fell on deaf ears.

The closing of the school

Davies was replaced by John Mockett Cramp (1796–1881), also a British Baptist, who served as principal till the College folded in 1849.[16] Since Davies was a vocal open communionist, it has been common to attribute the demise of the school to the conflict between open and closed communionists. This is certainly one reason for the school's failure, though other causes for its demise can be cited.

In 1849, Montreal was in the grip of a severe depression and that year there was a major cholera outbreak in the city, both of which discouraged potential students from coming to the College. The school had also been receiving support from British Baptist sources, but by 1849 this had completely dried up. Finally, there

---

14 "Ministerial Education," 198–199.
15 "Ministerial Education," 200.
16 On Cramp, see Robert S. Wilson, "Cramp, John Mockett." In *Blackwell Dictionary of Evangelical Biography*, Vol. 1, 266.

was the geographical isolation of the College from the bulk of the churches it was supposed to serve. Most of this constituency was between three- to six-hundred miles away to the west. It was impractical to expect ministerial students to journey that far in a day when transportation was exhausting and costly. For example, when John Girdwood, the pastor of the First Baptist Church in Montreal, travelled from Perth to Montreal in 1842, he had to "catch a stage at four a.m., travel over bone-shaking roads for many hours, then transfer to a river-boat to reach Montreal, the total journey occupying thirty-six hours."[17] The usual travelling time for a stage-coach from Toronto to Montreal was between ninety and one-hundred hours!

A coda

With the closure of Canada Baptist College, it would be a dozen years before the Ontario Baptist churches had another school of their own. The founding principal of that second school, the Canadian Literary Institute, would face similar challenges to those Davies encountered, but thankfully times were changing and the necessity of the school was increasingly recognized by Baptists in Ontario as the century wore on. Davies' reasons for having such a school, though, would remain as valid in the late nineteenth century as they were in 1840. And this author deems them to be still wisdom as we seek both "a learned" and "a pious ministry."

---

17 Theo T. Gibson, *Robert Alexander Fyfe: His Contemporaries and His Influence* (Burlington: Welch Publishing Co., 1998), 72.

03

Remembering the big picture: The backdrop to our preaching and teaching

BY BARRY HOWSON

One might consider this a rather ambitious title for one chapter in a book. But my goal for this chapter is simply to remind us that in our preaching and teaching ministries, the overall message of Scripture is God's plan of redemption for humanity and the world. From Genesis to Revelation, the purpose of the Scriptures is to reveal God's way of reconciliation, that is, to restore *shalom* that was lost at the fall and will be ultimately regained in the new heavens and the new earth. *Shalom* existed when God, in his love and grace, created humanity and placed Adam and Eve in Eden. There was perfect harmony between God and humans, between humans and humans and between God, humans and the universe. When humans rejected God's sovereign rule, harmony was lost, *shalom* was lost. All of Scripture from Genesis 3 through to Revelation 22 is God's revelation of how he will restore harmony and *shalom*.

In my early years as a pastor, I was quite aware of Scripture as the revelation of God's plan of redemption, but not in any clear and focused sense. This focus became sharper in the mid '90s when I read Don Carson's book, *The Gagging of God*.[1] In this work, Carson seeks to defend the truth of Christianity in the face of our modern and postmodern culture. At the end of the book, he gives some guidelines for the Christian and for the church in how to witness to this generation of particularly postmoderns. One of his points is that the church as a whole, and Christians individually, need to know what he called the "Biblical Plotline." He reasons that most people in our postmodern culture do not know who Jesus is and certainly don't know the background to the work of Christ. Consequently, in order to witness to this generation, we need to explain the biblical storyline from Creation to the Fall and then on to redemption. A few years later, a friend introduced me to Graeme Goldsworthy's book, *According to Plan*, which clearly articulated this biblical storyline.[2] Goldsworthy's book was very helpful in clearly delineating the biblical plotline. In my first years at Heritage College, I believed that it was important for our students to have this overall understanding of what Scripture is teaching from cover to cover. And so I developed a course which I entitled simply, "The Progress of Redemption." Out of all the courses that I teach, this is the one that has had the most profound effect upon students and one that they highly recommend to one another. It not only helps them to better articulate what the Scriptures teach to non-Christians, but maybe more importantly, strengthens their faith in the message of the Bible.

It is for this reason that I want to briefly share with you that which has been very helpful to me, and to many others, that is, the explication of God's great plan of redemption from the Bible's beginning to end. We need to be reminded that the Bible is not

---

[1] D.A. Carson, *The Gagging of God: Christianity Confronts Pluralism* (Grand Rapids: Zondervan, 2002).

[2] Graeme Goldsworthy, *According To Plan: The Unfolding Revelation of God in the Bible* (Downers Grove: IVP Academic, 2002).

primarily a book on morality or even how to live for God; it is primarily the unfolding of the grace of God to bring redemption to fallen humanity through his Son, Jesus Christ. Yes, the Bible does teach us how to please God with a life honouring him, but only on the basis of the salvation that has come through Christ and is applied to us through the work of the Holy Spirit. The centre of the Scripture is clearly God's grace through God's Son, Jesus Christ.

So then, what is this biblical plotline that declares the redemption of humanity and the world through Jesus Christ? It can be divided into three parts: creation, fall and redemption. One could look at it as three acts in a play. The first two acts are rather brief, taking up primarily the first three chapters of the Bible. It is the third act that takes up the rest of the Bible. If one were to continue with the illustration of a play, we could say that God is the producer, the director and the chief character. We could say that the hero of the story is his Son, Jesus Christ, and that the actors include the angels and humanity. We could further break down the last act into three parts or scenes. The first scene is "Redemption prophesied," which takes up the rest of the Old Testament. The second scene is "Redemption accomplished," which incorporates most of the New Testament and the last scene is "Redemption completed," which involves the final restoration of all things in a new heavens and new earth. In the rest of this essay, we will outline the basic contents of each act and each one of these final scenes. My hope is that this essay will encourage you to read books like Goldsworthy's to go deeper into this subject.

Act one: Creation

The first act of the biblical plot line we are calling "Creation," where *shalom* reigns on earth. There are various places throughout Scripture that address this first act, but the most important is Genesis 1 and 2. When Moses wrote these two chapters, he was teaching at least five truths. The first truth is that God, and in particular for the Israelites, YAHWEH, is the creator of the universe. This is evident from 1:1 that "in the beginning God created the heavens and the earth," depicting the creating of the whole universe. Moses makes clear that none of the other so-called gods of Egypt or any of the other nations created anything. It is the God of Israel who created all things. Second, it is evident from Genesis 1 that God created all things "good." This is repeated seven times in the passage which, for the Hebrews, was the number of perfection. The seventh time is found in verse 31, where it states, "God saw all that he had made, and it was very good." This would indicate to the Israelites that the evil that they saw around them was not part of the original creation. YAHWEH had made all things in the beginning "good," and as we might say, in "*shalom*," that is, in full harmony.

Third, Moses makes clear that God created humans as the pinnacle of his creation. This is evident in that humans were created on the sixth day as the culmination of his creation. In addition, it is stated in verse 26 that humans are made in God's image which is not stated of any other creation of God. There is certainly much debate about what this image of God means, but it is clear that whatever it means, it indicates that humans are special in God's creation. Moreover, their specialness is further evident in their call to subdue the earth and rule over it (v. 28). Also, the focus on Adam and Eve in chapter 2 enunciates their high place in God's creation, even in his communion and fellowship with them. From this the Israelites should understand that God has a special place for humans in his created world, and it should help them to see their importance in God's plan.

Fourth, the overall picture that Moses wants Israel to have of YAHWEH is that he is the sovereign Lord over his creation. He is the One who brought it all into being, and consequently, has the rightful place of ownership and rule. This is implicit in the passage but explicit in various places in the Scriptures, and in particular, in the Psalms.

Fifthly, Moses takes time to speak of what God did on the seventh day in Genesis 2:1–3, highlighting that *shalom* in God's creation is found in resting in him. We are utterly dependent upon him for all things, and we find our life, joy and satisfaction in him, and in him alone. This also would be a reminder to the Israelites, as they are making their way to the promised land, that they must trust in YAHWEH and depend upon him.

Act one is vital to a proper understanding of the rest of the Bible; in our witnessing of Christ, people need to understand that God created all things and originally all things were good, and that

God has made humans as the height of his creation to have fellow-ship with him. In addition they need to understand that he is the sovereign Lord over us and the one who supplies all our needs. There is no other.

Act two: Creation fallen

Act two, "Creation fallen," however, helps the Israelites and us understand why this world, presently has sin, death and corruption. God did not originally create it this way. So why is it now so? The answer is given in Genesis 3. Adam and Eve rejected God's lordship over their lives by disobeying God's one commandment to them. In light of act one, this is "the great rebellion," before which God had promised that if they disobeyed him, they would die. When they believed the temptation of the serpent, they disbelieved in God as Lord and provider, and so received the just recompense of their actions—death. This was death physical, spiritual and eternal. The physical aspect of death was not experienced immediately but, by the grace of God, much later in Adam's case. It was evident, however, in the death of Abel and again in the list of Adam's descendents in chapter 5 where we hear the constant refrain "and he died." The spiritual aspect of this death was separation and alienation from God which was evidenced in Adam and Eve's ejection from the garden and the presence of God. This spiritual death also included spiritual depravity, where hearts were no longer naturally desirous of God but desirous of sin and self. The eternal aspect of death occurs when a person who is spiritually dead, dies physically, which leads to eternal separation from God.

It should also be noted that chapter 3 provides answers to the problem of evil. Consequently, act two gives us the genesis of evil in our world that God originally created "good." It answers why there is both natural evil such as disease, destructive earthquakes, tsunamis, volcanoes, etc. (on account of Adam and Eve's disobedience to God, on the basis of which God cursed the very place that they were to rule and enjoy), and moral evil, that which humans commit against one another and against the creation itself. Instead of *shalom* reigning as God intended it to, now sin, Satan and death reign.

Act three: Creation redeemed

If we don't properly understand these first two acts, we can't truly understand act three, "Creation redeemed," which is the restoration of *shalom* in the plan of redemption accomplished through God's Son, Jesus Christ. So how does this third act begin? It begins with hope. The first scene of act three is the prophesying or foreshadowing of this redemption entitled, "Creation redeemed— prophesied." It begins immediately in Genesis 3 to 11, where God provides humans with great hope in spite of their fallenness. This hope is articulated in a several ways in these chapters. The first is the promise made in Genesis 3:15. It is spoken to the serpent, but within the hearing of the humans, that in light of what the serpent has done, he will be judged and crushed, and that this judgement will occur through a child of the woman who rebelled. Adam and Eve as well as Israel would understand by this that God was going to bring redemption to humanity through some human personage. This would have given them hope in the midst of their failure and lostness.

Another indication of hope given to humanity is found in the Noah narrative. Though humanity is deeply corrupt and progressively getting worse (Genesis 6:5), God is committed to redeeming humanity. He should have rightfully destroyed all of humanity but instead in his grace chose a handful of humans to continue his plan of redemption for humanity. The rainbow in the sky is the everlasting symbol of God's great grace and mercy to a rebellious humanity. It is a constant reminder to humans since the flood that our only hope is found in God and in his way of redemption. We must hang on to the promise of Genesis 3:15.

This scene of "Creation redeemed—prophesied" becomes more focused in Genesis 12 with the calling of Abraham. It will be through Abraham's line that the seed of the woman will crush the head of the serpent. Abraham in Genesis 12:1-7 is given four promises: descendents, blessing (God's presence), land and, most importantly, the blessing (brought into God's presence, reconciled to God) on all the nations of the earth through him. This is the promise that will be ultimately fulfilled in the second scene of act three with the coming of God's Son in the person of Jesus Christ, as Paul makes evident in Galatians 3 and 4. The rest of the first scene is the fleshing out of this promise, as the Old Testament foreshadows and prophesies its fulfillment.

There are two key points to this Abrahamic promise which are prophesied throughout the Old Testament and which will be fulfilled in Jesus. The first key point is that all nations will be blessed. This blessing is the restoration of *shalom* and communion with God, and a return to Eden for all humanity and for the universe. This is prophesied by the pre-exilic, exilic and postexilic prophets. For example, in Isaiah 2 Isaiah declares that

> In the last days the mountain of the Lord's temple will be established as the highest of the mountains; it will be exalted above the hills and *all nations* will stream to it. *Many peoples* will come and say, "Come let us go up to the mountain of the Lord to the Temple of the God of Jacob, he will teach us his ways so that we may walk in his paths"…[the nations] will beat their swords into plowshares and their spears into pruning hooks. Nation will not take up sword against nation [emphases mine].

And again in Isaiah 65, we are told that God will make a new heavens and a new earth where God will be in harmony with humanity, humanity with humanity, and humanity with the creation: a return to *shalom* for the universe (cf. vv. 17ff).

The second key point is that this will be accomplished through Abraham's seed, that is, a descendent of Abraham will accomplish this restoration of *shalom* and communion with God. And who is this seed? This first scene of act three proclaims that it will be a king. Just some of the verses that point to him as King include: Genesis 49:9–10; 2 Samuel 7:11–16; Isaiah 9:1–7, 11:1–11, 61:1–11; Jeremiah 23:5–6; Ezekiel 34:20–31; and Daniel 2 and 7. In particular, Isaiah 11 identifies this coming king as the one who will bring restoration to humanity and the universe.

However, to accomplish this salvation, this seed is not only a king but also a suffering servant. This is evident from Isaiah 42 to 53. In particular, in Isaiah 53, this servant of the Lord is the one who reconciles humanity, taking away its sin and death, through his own death, taking upon himself the punishment due to humanity. Moreover, this work of redemption through a suffering servant is also prophesied and foreshadowed in the Passover lamb that leads to the exodus, in the Levitical sacrifices and in the once-a-year event of the Day of Atonement.

The stage has been set for scene two of act three entitled, "Creation redeemed—accomplished." The prophecies of the first scene are fulfilled in the coming of the person and work of Jesus Christ. He is the prophesied King and Suffering Servant; this is evidenced in the Gospels in his birth, his public ministry and, most importantly, in his death and resurrection. In the birth narratives of Matthew and Luke, as well as the incarnation narrative of John's Gospel, we see that he is the King and the Son of God who is come to bring salvation to the world.

In Jesus' public ministry, it is evident that he is the messianic king by his defeat of humanity's enemies. We see him defeating sin in the granting of the forgiveness of sins in Mark 2. We see it in his defeat of Satan as he goes about casting out demons, and even seeing Satan falling from heaven. And lastly, we see in his public ministry his victory over death by the raising of people from the dead including Lazarus, Jairus' daughter, and the widow of Nain's son. In his public ministry he is demonstrating that he is the Messiah King who has come to conquer humanity's enemies. He has come to destroy the reign of sin, Satan and death which entered the world so long ago, and that God promised to destroy.

We see the defeat and the conquering of sin, Satan and death at the cross and resurrection of Jesus Christ. Consequently, when Jesus Christ rises from the dead, he is the first human since Adam to be free of sin, Satan and death. He is the first human of the new creation, of restored *shalom*. This is not the end of scene two; this new creation advances through the work of the Holy Spirit, beginning with his coming at Pentecost in Acts 2, and spreading throughout humanity and throughout the world even to this day. This is why Jesus can say that he is building his church and the gates of Hades will not prevail against it. The whole world is in captivity to death, and the gospel is advancing, taking captives captive to itself, restoring humanity to its proper place of *shalom* with God.

But not all is completed yet and so scene three is necessary: "Creation redeemed—completed," which takes place after the return of Jesus Christ. This is to what Jesus refers when speaking of the regeneration of all things (Matthew 19), and to which Peter refers when he speaks about the destruction of the old heavens and earth and the creating of a new heavens and earth (2 Peter 3). This third scene is the completion of the redeemed creation. This is depicted, not in great detail, but certainly with clarity in the last chapters of the book of Revelation where God's enemies are destroyed in chapters 19 and 20; sin, Satan and death are no more, and, as we see in Revelation 21 and 22, there is a return to Edenic life in the presence of God where *shalom* has been restored in full.

Final thoughts

This is what the Bible is all about. The key to interpreting all of Scripture is God's plan of redemption through the person and work of Jesus Christ. As Jesus himself said to his disciples after his resurrection, "This is what I told you while I was still with you: everything must be fulfilled that is written about me in the law of Moses, the prophets and the Psalms. Then he opened their minds so they could understand the Scriptures" (Luke 24:44).

My hope is that this brief look at God's plan of redemption, the story of the Bible, will encourage us to think more deeply about it and read more about it and so, in turn, it will better inform our preaching and teaching ministries.[3]

---

3 For those of you who are interested in reading further on this subject, here are several suggestions:

- Graeme Goldsworthy, *According To Plan: The Unfolding Revelation of God in the Bible* (Downers Grove: IVP Academic, 2002).
- Vaughan Roberts, *God's Big Picture: Tracing the Storyline of the Bible* (Downers Grove: IVP, 2003).
- Craig G. Bartholomew and Michael W. Goheen, *The Drama of Scripture: Finding our Place in the Biblical Story* (Grand Rapids: Baker Academic, 2004).

And, in particular for preachers and teachers, I highly recommend Graeme Goldsworthy's *Preaching the Whole Bible as Christian Scripture: The Application of Biblical Theology to Expository Preaching* (Grand Rapids: Eerdmanns, 2000). Here he shows how to read and preach Scripture from a plan of redemption perspective.

04

Recovering the metaphor of shepherd in pastoral leadership and ministry

BY DAVID BARKER

Introduction

Eugene Peterson in his book, *The Pastor*, writes:

> North American culture does not offer congenial conditions in which to live vocationally as a pastor. [Pastors]...find that they have entered a way of life that is in ruins. The vocation of pastor has been replaced by the strategies of religious entrepreneurs with business plans. Any kind of continuity with pastors in times past is virtually non-existent.
>
> ...I don't love the rampant consumerism that treats God as a product to be marketed. In don't love the dehumanizing ways that turn men, women, and children into impersonal roles and causes and statistics.... The cultural conditions in

which I am immersed require, at least for me, a kind of fierce vigilance to guard my vocation from these cultural pollutants so dangerously toxic to persons who want to follow Jesus in the way that is Jesus. I wanted my life, both my personal and working life, to be shaped by God and the scriptures and prayer.[1]

In recent times, in concert with Peterson's observations, a surprising idea about pastoring has emerged; namely, it is time to abandon the biblical metaphor of "shepherd" to describe who and what a pastor is and does. Andy Stanley, when asked the question, "Should we stop talking about pastors as shepherds?" in a *Leadership* magazine interview, replied, "Absolutely. The word needs to go away…. It was culturally relevant in the time of Jesus, but it's not culturally relevant anymore."[2]

All across the evangelical church in North America, in the demand for "leadership," we are seeing pastors donning the mantle of corporate president, and lapsing into the world of power, position, management and control.

Reflections

Several things come to mind in response. First, it is difficult to retain the name "pastor" and abandon the idea of shepherd. The word for pastor in the New Testament, *poiema*, means "shepherd." Therefore, those who go down this path must choose another more suitable term to describe themselves other than "pastor."

Second, it means that we somehow have to work around the texts in which the word and idea occurs, and the implication that it continues to inform what we do as pastors. The Apostle Paul writes, "It was Christ who gave some to be apostles, some to be prophets, some to be evangelists, and some to be pastors [shepherds] and teachers" (Ephesians 4:11). The apostle Peter writes, "To the elders among you, I appeal as a fellow elder, a witness of Christ's sufferings and one who will also share in the glory to be revealed: Be *shepherds* of God's flock that is under your care" (1 Peter 5:2).

---

1 Eugene Peterson, *The Pastor: A Memoir* (New York: HarperCollins, 2011), 4–5.
2 Andy Stanley, "State of the Art," *Leadership* (Spring 2006): 28.

Third, the metaphor has been part of the language of the church for over 2,000 years. It is doubtful that we have come to the place where we have the power and privilege to declare the idea as irrelevant. Urban life has existed throughout history since the times of the New Testament.

Finally, when we explore the metaphor biblically, we find that it captures the necessary ideas of pastoral care and leadership that make the task and duties of a pastor work. The following is a start to that exploration.

The idea of shepherd in Scripture[3]

1. Shepherds are leaders.

There is no loss of the idea of shepherd as a leader in Scripture. God, as a shepherd, led his people out of Egypt (Psalm 78:52–55). Moses "led God's people like a flock" (Psalm 77:20). David was anointed to be a shepherd-king, a ruler, fully a king, but a shepherd (2 Samuel 5:1–3; Ezekiel 34:23; 37:24–25).

In the Ancient Near East, Babylonian and Assyrian kings, such as Hammurabi and Tiglath-Pileser I, were called shepherds or shepherd-kings. This concept informs Psalm 23:1, "The LORD is my "shepherd [-king]." That is why we have the picture of a palace banquet hall in verse five. We have moved from the pastures to the king's palace.

If we are worried that the notion of a shepherd is only some kind of passive, gentle, lamb-carrying figure, it is quickly corrected by observing strong leaders in the Old Testament and the Ancient Near East called shepherds.

2. Shepherds bring their people home from exile.

This signifies mission, and it is a passionate and purposeful one.

While Isaiah 40:11 captures the tender care and compassion of a shepherd ("lambs in his arms," "carries them close to his heart"), the picture that informs this text starts in Isaiah 40:1 with the call

---

3 I have used Timothy S. Laniak, *Shepherds after My Own Heart: Pastoral Traditions and Leadership in the Bible.* Vol. 20. *New Studies in Biblical Theology*, ed. D.A Carson (Downers Grove: InterVarsity Press, 2006) as a base upon which to develop my thoughts in the remaining material.

to comfort God's people, to announce that their hard service is over and that there is a voice calling in the wilderness, "Prepare the way of the LORD."

Shepherds are the proclaimers and leaders of the second exodus. They inspire hope, announcing, facilitating and leading restoration, healing and homecoming. They bring people from the kingdom of darkness (Babylon) to the kingdom of God's dear Son (Colossians 1:13).

The shepherd's task is missional. It involves rescue and return. It is bringing men and women, boys and girls, by repentance and faith in Jesus Christ, into the now-but-not-yet kingdom of God. This is the gospel, and the shepherd's mission is that gospel.

3. Shepherds are to be committed to the care and protection of the flock.

This idea is everywhere in the Scriptures. We've already seen it in Isaiah 40:11. Psalm 23 describes the Lord's care for the flock. The prophet Zechariah, in chapter 11, rebukes the shepherds who use the sheep for their own prosperity, and twice in Ezekiel 34, God pronounces woe against the shepherds who do not care for the flock. Tending the flock was the core responsibility of the shepherd.

We call it "soul care," care for souls, and it is hard, slow, often unmeasurable work. Sometimes the stories can't be told, and can't be recorded in our reports to our elders and annual meetings because of confidentialities. But long, slow, patient, steady soul care is the task of a pastor.

4. Sometimes shepherds need to rebuke and discipline the flock.

In Zechariah 11:7-14, we have the shepherd breaking the staffs called Favour and Union. God, as shepherd, breaks the flock apart and removes his grace. As under-shepherds, we may be called to exercise a similar kind of discipline in our congregations. However, the process to reach this point would need to be excruciatingly painful, deeply prayerful, and dominated by wisdom, counsel and care.

5. Shepherds may be called upon to suffer for the purification of the flock.

When we look at Zechariah 13:7–9, we find that it is the true shepherd who is struck for the sake of the redemption of the sheep. Jesus picks the image up in Mark 14:27 and Matthew 26:31 and applies it to his sacrifice on the cross.

I would suggest that this also speaks to the role and task of the under-shepherd. As under-shepherds of the Arch-Shepherd, we are called to the same. As servants of the suffering Servant, we are called to be the suffering servant in the world and church. In John 10:11, Jesus says that "The good shepherd lays down his life for the sheep," and that idea overflows into the task and mission of pastors.

6. Shepherds were marginalized and despised, not part of the social elite.

Have we ever noticed that it was shepherds who visited the Christ-child first? Luke recounts this part of the story to send the message to the church that it was the poor and marginalized who recognized the Messiah at Bethlehem, not the nobility and religious elite. When pastors are identified as shepherds, we are identified with people in the margins of social acceptance.

In 1 Samuel 16, David is the eighth (the oops) of Jesse's perfect number of seven sons. He is called the *qaton*, the "little one." He is the one tending the sheep while the rest of the brothers were eligible for kingship. Tending sheep was the job for the *qaton*.

As shepherds, we serve the church and society from the margins of power and position. In doing so, we follow the One who had no place to lay his head.

7. Shepherds are responsible to seek and to save the lost one.

Luke 15:4–7 tells us the famous story of the one-out-of-a-hundred lost sheep. The point of the story is that in the kingdom of God finding and restoring one lost sheep is cause for rejoicing. The shepherd in the kingdom of God is prepared to abandon the rest in the open country, to find the one!

When pastors become more enthralled with the many, the established community, the people with power and entitlement, and abandon the search for the one, the lost one, perhaps a marginalized and powerless one, we have lost the ministry of shepherd.

8. Shepherds are intimately known and trusted by the sheep.

From John 10:1–5, we understand that the sheep hear the shepherd's voice and they do follow. Their response is rooted in trust: proven character, care and sacrifice on the part of the shepherd.

The incentive for a congregation to follow is not the position, title or office: Pastor, Reverend, Doctor. It is their shepherd's care for them.

Years ago, I heard this in a pastoral theology class: "For the first three years you are their preacher, for the next three years you become their pastor, and only after that do you become their leader." There is no entitlement attached to the title "pastor," no presumptuous expectation that the flock will follow. For shepherds to be intimately known and trusted by the sheep requires unhurried time, unhurried conversations, unhurried journeying together.

9. Shepherds show shepherd-care for their flock rooted in love for Christ.

In John 21:15–22, we have the famous *agape* and *phileo* interchange between Peter and Jesus. Simon, do you *agape* me? Feed my lambs. Simon, do you *agape* me? Feed my sheep. Simon, do you *phileo* me? Feed my sheep. Whether it is *agape* or *phileo*, he wants Peter to love him in heart, mind, decision and passion.

So, while there is care and love for the flock, there is even more care and love for the Shepherd of the flock whom we serve as under-shepherds. We start with passion for God, and out of the overflow of that passion, we minister as shepherds to the lambs and sheep.

This presupposes that we spend time with Christ in prayer, that we devote ample time to study and reflection on Scripture and that we live our lives in obedience to the Word.

The place where we as pastors work needs to be called our "study," not our "office." Offices are places where presidents, corporate executives and administrators work. Pastors do their work in their study.

10. Shepherds live out a servant, sacrificial spirit.
1 Peter 5:1–4 talks about being eager to serve, not lording over, living as examples, not greedy for money and eager to serve. Jesus, in Matthew and Mark, said that the call of the kingdom is "not so with you." Christ's kingdom is diametrically opposed to the power models of Gentile rule (cf. Mark 10:35–45).

David Hansen, in his book *The Art of Pastoring: Ministry without All the Answers*, writes this:

> Jesus specifically directed us to follow him in his life's general direction, the Way of the Cross. Lest we object to bearing the cross as pietistic nonsense in a world of "scientific" management principles and psychological method, simply observe that all the trouble the best, most talented pastors get into comes from not following the Way of the Cross. The best and most talented in the pastoral ministry and in denominational hierarchies harm themselves and harm the church most through their unrestrained ego and unwillingness to step out of the high places. Sexual sin gets the press, but ego sin kills the church.[4]

Summary and reflections

So while some are prepared to abandon the idea of shepherd in pastoral ministry, which in itself is a contradiction, we need to recover the metaphor of pastor as shepherd with all the implications that we have talked about above. We as pastors, our congregations, and our elders, boards and leaders, all need to understand this.

Eugene Peterson tells the story of a gathering of a group of about fifteen pastors that met every Tuesday morning to reflect on Scripture, church and pastoral ministry. They were called "The Company of Pastors." He writes:

> We wanted to clarify for ourselves, even if not for others, what was unique about us as pastors. We were tired of letting people who were not pastors tell us what we should be doing or not

---

4 David Hansen, *The Art of Pastoring: Ministry without All the Answers* (Downers Grove: InterVarsity Press, 1994), 27.

be doing as pastors. The sociologists and academics, the psychologists and business executives, the talk-show gurus and religious entrepreneurs, had all had their say long enough.[5]

The apostle Peter issues the call: "Be shepherds of God's flock. Eager to serve, not lording it over those entrusted to you, but being examples to the flock. And when the Chief Shepherd appears, you will receive the garland of glory that will never fade away" (1 Peter 5:2–4). It is time to elevate Scripture to its rightful place, and embrace our pastoral/shepherding calling and vocation even more vigorously than ever before.

---

5   Peterson, *The Pastor*, 146.

05

Minding the gap: Why background matters for preaching and teaching

BY WAYNE BAXTER

One of the fundamental doctrines of evangelical Christianity is the perspicuity of Scripture: essentially, that the Bible is clear and understandable. This doctrine is one of the working assumptions for the ministry of preaching and teaching. When I served as a youth pastor, I used to preach expositional messages from the Bible to my youth (albeit briefly, and with loads of offbeat, youth pastor humour), on the one hand; and I strongly encouraged my students to read the Bible regularly (i.e. that they "do devotions"), on the other. Why? Because I assumed that my young audience could understand the sacred text for themselves: the perspicuity of Scripture. But if the words of the Bible are clear and understandable, does it follow that we can confidently ignore studying the social-historical background of a passage (after all, the Bible is clear and understandable)? Moreover, why even study the background of the Bible since Scripture and Scripture alone is divinely revealed, divinely inspired and inerrant for faith and practice?

Understanding Scripture's view of understanding Scripture

Protestant evangelicals rightly believe that every Christian can read and understand the Bible for him or herself. Yet Scripture itself also implicitly affirms that its perspicuity does not eliminate the problem of having only a partial understanding of God's Word. Numerous injunctions to meditate on God's laws (eg, Joshua 1:8; Psalm 1:2) presuppose that the believer's comprehension of God's Word can and must grow deeper over time. Nor does the Bible's perspicuity do away with the possibility of completely misunderstanding Scripture. The apostle Peter acknowledges that some of what Paul writes is "hard to understand" (2 Peter 3:16a), and consequently, some people "distort [his teaching], as they do the other Scriptures" (2 Peter 3:16b). Neither does Scripture's perspicuity remove the necessity of teachers in the church. The fact that God has given some believers the spiritual gift of teaching (see 1 Corinthians 12:28–29; Romans 12:7) and has appointed the ecclesial office of teaching within the church (see Ephesians 4:11–12) plainly presupposes that not everyone will understand God's Word well without some human assistance.

Clearly, then, although Scripture has the capability of being rightly understood by all, not everyone understands it accurately. Is there something that can help bolster our knowledge of the Bible?

Meaning: Recognizing the need for context

One of the most common mantras pertaining to understanding Scripture is "the plain, literal meaning of the text." When reading the Bible it is always best to take the plain, literal meaning of the text. But given the complexity of the Bible, is it always that simple? A straightforward, contemporary example can illustrate the difficulty: "I love this course." What do those four words mean? Is it not simply a matter of taking the plain, literal meaning of those four words? No. There is more to it. If those words were uttered by one of my students at Heritage Seminary, then s/he would clearly be expressing what they think of my class (and who could blame them for feeling that way?). If they were spoken by Chef Gordon Ramsay, then he would probably be referring to some food course like Beef Wellington (since he has never had me as a prof). If the words came from Tiger Woods or Jack Nicklaus (who again, have never been my students), then they would be talking about something else: a golf course, like Augusta or Pebble Beach. But what if a student said those words—God forbid—sarcastically? Then that simple, four-word statement would actually mean the opposite: "I don't like this course!" The plain, literal meaning of those four words can denote entirely different things, depending on who is speaking and to whom they are speaking—in other words, depending on their *social-historical context*.

Context: Minding the gap
The inescapable fact of the matter is this: modern readers of the Bible find themselves in an *interpretative gap*. *Language* contributes to this gap. Neither David, nor Isaiah, nor Paul wrote their texts in English (King James or otherwise). The texts of Scripture were originally written in either ancient Hebrew, Aramaic or Greek. People proficient in more than one language can easily attest that meaning often gets "lost in translation." For example, when someone has an inexplicable tickle in their throat impeding their ability to speak at that moment, the person commonly says, "I have a frog in my throat." This idiomatic expression could never be translated literally into French because the native French speaker would think that the person is choking on a bite of frog legs. The French equivalent of this English expression would be, "I have a cat in my throat." And conversely, a literal translation of this French idiom into English would conjure up for the native English speaker images of icky fur balls in someone's throat. Translating between languages is not simple, and things—like important nuances and shades of meaning—often get lost in translation. Modern readers of the Bible are in a language gap that obstructs the clarity of the Bible.

Time adds to this interpretive gap. Neither Moses, nor Jeremiah, nor Matthew wrote their texts recently. The youngest or most recent text of Scripture was written over nineteen hundred years ago. The difficulty that this presents is that the meanings of words change over time. In 1611, the venerable King James Version translated the Hebrew text of Genesis 2:24 as, "Therefore shall a man leave his father and his mother, and shall cleave unto his wife: and they shall be one flesh." While the word "cleave" meant "unite" in the seventeenth century, four hundred years later the word "cleave" now has the exact opposite meaning. Butchers, for example, do not use meat "cleavers" to join meat together but to separate meat from bones and tendons. In chemistry, ionic lattices "cleave," meaning, they split apart not come together. The common understanding of a word can change significantly even within one generation. Today, if someone says the word "cell," everyone assumes cell phone. But just thirty years ago, no one would ever have made that association. People would have thought of a prison cell, or a skin cell, or part of an organism. Words can and often do take on different meanings over time. The fact that modern readers are separated from the texts of Scripture by a time gap of some two or three millennia invariably obscures the clarity of the Bible.

Cultural norms increase this interpretive gap. Neither Ezra, nor Hosea, nor Luke operated out of our twenty-first century Western cultural norms. Our North American or Western cultural value of individualism, for example, fails at first blush to comprehend the nature of the father-son relationship in the ancient world. For the ancients, sons were expected to follow in their father's footsteps vocationally. That is why, for example, Amos, when he seeks to emphasize the veracity of his prophetic call, can declare, "I was neither a prophet nor a prophet's son, but I was a shepherd, and I also took care of sycamore-fig trees" (Amos 7:14). Only the son of a prophet could be expected to become a prophet. When Jesus in John's Gospel, then, speaks of God as his Father and refers to himself as God's Son, it is not that this only implies an ontological equivalence,[1] but rather, a functional one. In other words, it is precisely because Jesus is God's true Son that he can do everything that the Father does (cf. John 5:19–23). Unrecognized differences in cultural values and norms heighten the interpretive

---

1   In the Old Testament, God, for example, can refer to the nation of Israel as well as to the king as his "son" (cf. Exodus 4:22 and 2 Samuel 7:14, respectively).

gap for the modern reader of the Bible and thus, cloud the clarity of Scripture.

Another factor that enlarges this interpretive gap is the matter of *shared history and experiences*. When the modern reader comes to a text, s/he approaches it as a blank slate, insofar as knowing the people and their specific situation that the biblical author seeks to address. The author, however, was anything but a blank slate when he sought to help his original audience. He never wrote his text in a social-historical vacuum. Often the biblical author was extremely familiar with his first audience and his experience with them shaped what he said to them. The shared experiences between the author and his audience, invariably enabled the biblical author to write things in a shorthand or crib notes kind of way that his first audience would have understood immediately. But subsequent readers would not, because they lack this shared history.

Some time after I graduated from seminary, I received a letter from one of my close seminary chums, Jeff. Jeff's letter ended with this postscript: "Tell Justin I found a copy of Benny Hester's *Run to You*." To anyone who read that letter but lacked our shared experience, that sentence would simply wash over them. But to the reader privy to our shared history, that postscript would cause them to laugh hysterically because that statement was a joke—something not clear from the plain, literal meaning of those words. Only access to the shared history between Jeff and me could reveal the joke. Modern Bible readers find themselves in an interpretive gap because they lack the shared experiences that existed between the biblical author and his original audience; and this lack of knowledge blurs the clarity of Scripture.

While the Bible is clear and comprehendible, the doctrine of the perspicuity of Scripture surely does not preclude the notion of understanding through effort and the use of ordinary means.[2] The study of social-historical backgrounds comprises an integral part of the effort and ordinary means necessary to narrow this wide interpretive gap between the modern reader and the Bible and thus,

---

2 See Wayne Grudem's nuanced definition of "perspicuity" in his conference paper, "The Perspicuity of Scripture," *Tyndale Fellowship Conference: The John Wenham Lecture*, Cambridge University, July 2009.

to understand Scripture accurately. But besides meaning, is there something else at stake in the use or disuse of background studies?

Context: Making the natural connections

Reading does not equal understanding. Any native English speaker could pick up and read flawlessly any page from my Ph.D. dissertation, pronouncing all of the (English) words correctly. But would that person understand anything of what s/he just read? Probably not, because my highly technical dissertation was written for biblical scholars. Reading does not equal understanding. Understanding is the necessary next step to reading. The study of social-historical backgrounds represents the next step to reading the text. But social-historical context is not just a matter of meaning, it is also a matter of drawing the proper connections between the text and the reader, that is, *application*.

Homileticians of every stripe have always preached, "Application, application, application." Lay people crave application. But is all application sound application? In moving from text to interpreter some verses proceed in a fairly straight-line manner. This is true especially of the New Testament letters (although some parts of them are not like this). Paul, for example, tells the Philippians: "Do nothing out of selfish ambition or vain conceit. Rather, in humility value others above yourselves, not looking to your own interests but each of you to the interests of the others" (Philippians 2:3–4). While the Greek would provide important nuances to understanding these verses, applying them, nevertheless, seems straightforward enough: as Christians go about their lives they need to figure out ways that they can look out for their brothers and sisters and not just for themselves.

But while letters often proceed in this straight-line manner to application, narratives are a different story. When a person turns to Christ for salvation, when can that new believer expect to receive the Holy Spirit? According to Acts, the answer to this question is varied. Acts 2:37–41 speaks of the promise of the Spirit coming to those who repent and are baptized. Acts 8:5–17 says that the new believers received the Spirit only after the apostles laid hands on them and not after their baptism. Acts 10:34–48 describes how the Gentiles received the Holy Spirit prior to being baptized and without the laying on of apostolic hands. The book of Acts presents contradictory answers to this question—contradictory, that is, if the reader tries to move in a straight-line manner from text to application. But with narratives (as well as with other genres of Scripture), straight-line application simply does not work. While the stories of the Bible record theological history, they do not record theology in a systematic form. The writers of biblical narratives understand history theologically, and consequently their stories have definite theological underpinnings; yet their stories function first and foremost as stories not as theological treatises. Application in these cases proceeds in a less direct, and a more dotted-line fashion. The study of social-historical background enables the reader to discern more readily when application is a straight-line and when it should proceed in a dotted-line manner. Making this central distinction helps the reader to draw sound, natural connections for applying the text rather than loose, highly artificial ones.

Context: Using the right connections

While everyone can surely benefit from graduate biblical studies, most people—pastors and laity alike—have neither the time nor the money nor the energy to invest in further, formal studies in order to become biblical scholars. Moreover, the field of biblical scholarship is so fantastically broad that no scholar has expertise in all of its sub-disciplines, and few scholars have genuine proficiency in a lot of areas. So then, how does someone go about reading and deploying material from an area in which s/he has never been trained? The simple answer is *commentaries*. Commentators have already done most of the heavy lifting. It is imperative, however, that the right kind of commentaries be employed. The best commentaries for evangelical pastors and lay people to pursue background studies possess two chief characteristics.[3] First, they are *evangelical*. While there are many excellent background studies done by non-evangelicals, frequently many helpful insights become embedded in bad theology; or good insights lead to poor, heterodoxical or even heretical conclusions. Most Christians readily recognize this danger and freely abide by this first maxim.

---

3 For an excellent resource for selecting commentaries, see D.A. Carson, *New Testament Commentary Survey* (Grand Rapids: Baker, 2001).

A second characteristic of the best commentaries is that they are *academic*. Here is where many Christian libraries fall short. Most pastors and lay people settle for devotional commentaries or pastoral commentaries or homiletical commentaries. While these types of commentaries have their use, they simply remain inadequate to provide solid background studies for at least the following reasons. First, while these commentators have some capability in the original languages, their proficiency still falls far short of where it needs to be to deal skillfully with background studies. Second, their academic or theological training is narrowly focused on Scripture and does not really include significant work in the area of the social-historical background of the Bible. Third, their deeply ingrained theological prejudices keep them from dealing with background material in an even-handed way. Admittedly, academic commentaries demand more from their audience: they tend to be a bit technical (and there are no pictures!). But the extra effort it takes to digest what they offer is well worth their higher ticket price. Some of the more helpful academically oriented (or "semi-technical") commentary series include the *Baker Exegetical Commentary on the New Testament*, the *Pillar New Testament Commentary*, the updated version of the *New International Commentary* and the *New American Commentary*. It should be noted, however, that as with any series, some individual volumes are better than others.

Conclusion

The Bible is God's divinely revealed, divinely inspired and inerrant Word. Because it is clear and understandable, we must continue to preach and teach it to our people, and encourage them to read and study it for themselves. Nevertheless, Scripture is an ancient, foreign and complex text; and these qualities create an interpretive gap for modern readers—a gap which results in many Christians having, despite Scripture's perspicuity, a partial understanding of God's Word, or in some cases, a complete misunderstanding of it. By digging into the social-historical backgrounds of Scripture, we can narrow this interpretive gap so as to deepen our understanding of God's Word and apply it properly to our lives, in order to become more like Jesus, the Word-made-flesh.

06

(Not)hearing God: Leadership lessons from the book of Judges

BY GORD OESTE

I was scrolling through the list of the top twenty most read religious news postings of 2014 on the *Christianity Today* website and was struck by how many of the top postings were connected in some way to missteps taken by Christian leaders.[1] The list included people along the entire spectrum of evangelical leaders who had powerful ministries that impacted the lives of many. And yet, somewhere along the way, something happened and these leaders made decisions that I'm sure they deeply regret now. The part that grabbed me was that in each of these cases, none of

---

[1] *Christianity Today* website (http://www.christianitytoday.com/gleanings/2014/december/top-20-most-read-gleanings-of-2014-christianity-today.html; accessed January 5, 2015).

the people started by turning their backs on God and walking away from the faith. Instead, somewhere along the line, these godly leaders with good leadership track records slid off into some very poor decision-making. At first, I began to ask myself: How did that happen? How did they end up at a point where they are making North American religious headlines, for all the wrong reasons? After further reflection, I realized that this is not anything new, but has happened many times in the history of the church and goes all the way back to the days of Israel in the Old Testament. In fact, it brought to mind a reality that is rarely noticed in the book of Judges.

1. The downward spiral in Judges

The book of Judges is set in the period of Israel's history just before the advent of Israel's kings.[2] The book has two parallel introductions (1:1–2:5; 2:6–3:6) that set the book just after the death of Joshua. What follows are cycles of stories that describe how God raised up numerous deliverers to rescue Israel (3:7–16:31), though a better visual image might be a downward spiral, so that the further you read in the book of Judges, the worse things get. The best judge in the book of Judges is Othniel (3:7–11) and, by far, the worst is Samson (13:1–16:31). Just when you think things couldn't sink any lower with Samson, the last judge in Judges,[3] the book ends with two final episodes where there are no judges, and complete and utter moral and spiritual chaos follows (17:1–18:31; 19:1–21:25), punctuated by the repeated observation that "there was no king in the land, and everyone did what was right in their own eyes" (17:6; 21:25).[4]

The moral and spiritual breakdown in the period of the judges seems complete when a Levite is almost assaulted and his concubine, along with the daughter of their host, is brutally gang-raped

---

[2] Two commentaries that I've found very helpful for both their exegetical sensitivity and theological insight are: Daniel I. Block, *Judges, Ruth* (NAB; Nashville: Broadman & Holman, 1999) and K. Lawson Younger, *Judges/Ruth* (NIVAC; Grand Rapids: Zondervan, 2002).

[3] While Samson is the last judge named in the book of Judges, it is actually Samuel who serves as the last of Israel's judges (see 1 Samuel 7:15–16).

[4] All quotations taken from the NIV 2011.

all night long by the men of Gibeah (Judges 19). Israel is rightly outraged and vows to punish the perpetrators (20:10), massing for war against the city of Gibeah. The rest of the Benjamites side with their kinfolk, the people of Gibeah, which leads to a complete collapse of national unity and devolves into an Israelite civil war.

Israel does not lightly enter into this battle against one of their fellow Israelite tribes (the Benjamites), but asks the LORD's counsel: "The Israelites went up to Bethel and inquired of God. They said, 'Who of us is to go up first to fight against the Benjamites?' The LORD replied, 'Judah shall go first'" (20:18). Curiously, all Israel fights, and seemingly the LORD's counsel leads to the slaughter of 22,000 Israelites and a Benjamite victory. Israel again inquires of the LORD: "The Israelites went up and wept before the LORD until evening, and they inquired of the LORD. They said, 'Shall we go up again to fight against the Benjamites, our fellow Israelites?' The LORD answered, 'Go up against them'" (20:23). Once again, 18,000 Israelites are mowed down in defeat. Israel inquires of the LORD a third time:

> Then all the Israelites, the whole army, went up to Bethel, and there they sat weeping before the LORD. They fasted that day until evening and presented burnt offerings and fellowship offerings to the LORD. And the Israelites inquired of the LORD. (In those days the ark of the covenant of God was there, with Phinehas son of Eleazar, the son of Aaron, ministering before it.) They asked, "Shall we go up again to fight against the Benjamites, our fellow Israelites, or not?" The LORD responded, "Go, for tomorrow I will give them into your hands" (Judges 20:26–28).

Finally, after the third try, Israel is successful. Too successful, in fact, and they nearly wipe out the entire Benjamite tribe before they realize at the last minute what they have done and blame God for their actions:

> The men of Israel had taken an oath at Mizpah: "Not one of us will give his daughter in marriage to a Benjamite." The people went to Bethel, where they sat before God until evening,

raising their voices and weeping bitterly. "LORD, God of Israel," they cried, "*why has this happened to Israel? Why should one tribe be missing from Israel today?*" (Judges 21:1–3, emphasis mine)

In a study of the complete breakdown portrayed in the book of Judges, Old Testament scholar Cheryl Exum proposes that God is very intimately involved in the chaos depicted in the book. Twice, inquiry of the LORD leads to Israel's military defeat and the LORD's final OK almost leads to the elimination of one of the twelve tribes of Israel. This is just the capstone on the breakdown that we see throughout the book of Judges, and Exum concludes, "In Judges 17–21, YHWH's rule is ineffectual, either because YHWH does not intervene in events or because YHWH intervenes in ways that result in destruction rather than benefit. YHWH thus shares with Israel responsibility for the disorder with which Judges ends."[5]

Exum's comment seems out of line. The LORD's counsel is mentioned in conjunction with the chaos at the end of the book, but does God really share responsibility for the disorder we find at the end of the book of Judges? Is he really part of the problem in Judges as Exum holds?

One of the hermeneutical keys to understanding what we read in the book of Judges is the observation we made earlier that events in the book of Judges are basically set out in a downward spiral. This means that the further we read in Judges, the greater the moral and spiritual breakdown. If we read with this in mind, I think we can gain a helpful perspective on the chaos at the end of the book of Judges, and so better understand what is happening when God's counsel seems to feed the civil war between the Benjamites and the Israelites.

2. Not listening—The introduction to Judges

The book of Judges begins with the Israelites asking virtually the same question regarding the Canaanites that they ask in Judges 20 about the Benjamites: "After the death of Joshua, the Israel-

---

5 J. Cheryl Exum, "The Centre Cannot Hold: Thematic and Textual Instabilities in Judges." In *Reconsidering Israel and Judah: Recent Studies on the Deuteronomistic History* eds. Gary N. Knoppers and J. Gordon McConville (Winona Lake: Eisenbrauns, 2000), 600. Originally published in *CBQ* 52 (1990): 410–431.

ites asked the LORD, 'Who of us is to go up first to fight against the Canaanites?' The LORD answered, 'Judah shall go up; I have given the land into their hands'" (1:1–2). But Judah immediately fails to take God at his word and invites Simeon to join in their battles. And that little compromise sets the tone for the rest of the book. Throughout Judges, Israel increasingly fails to listen to the LORD. Judah and Simeon are by far the most successful tribes at carrying out the task of taking possession of the land, but even they do not take on the cities of the plain (1:19). The rest of the tribes are increasingly unsuccessful and compromise by making covenants with the Canaanites, so that when God sends his angel to chastise Israel, the angel highlights Israel's refusal to listen the LORD, "You shall not make a covenant with the people of this land, but you shall break down their altars. Yet you have disobeyed [or you did not listen to] me. Why have you done this?" (2:2). The second "introduction" to the book of Judges (2:6–3:6) highlights a similar problem, saying, "They would not listen to their judges" (2:17) and Israel "has not listened to me" (2:20). These early failures set in motion a pattern that is repeatedly highlighted throughout the next section of the book of Judges: Israel's growing failure to listen to the LORD, as increasingly reflected in the lives of their leaders, the judges.

3. Not listening—Israel's Judges

Israel's willingness to listen to the LORD seems to get a good start as the first two judges (Othniel, 3:7–11; Ehud, 3:12–30) do not exhibit any of the recalcitrance that will plague the later judges. But things change with Israel's third judge, Barak (4:1–5:31). When Barak is told by God's prophetess, Deborah, to marshal Israel's tribes to fight against Jabin, the king of Hazor, Barak refuses to obey the LORD's commission (4:8) unless Deborah goes with him. When Deborah agrees to accompany Barak (4:9), he willingly does what God asked him to do, but because of his hesitancy, the honour for the victory goes to a non-Israelite woman named Jael (4:9, 21–22; 5:24–27).

Israel's willingness to listen to the LORD goes further off the rails in the story of the next judge, Gideon, and his son Abimelech (6:1–9:57). At the beginning of the Gideon story, an unnamed prophet reminds Israel that they were not to worship other gods concluding, "But you have not listened to me" (6:10). The story then moves on to Gideon who exhibits a heightened unwilling-ness to listen to God. While Barak responded immediately after Deborah said she would accompany him into battle, Gideon is the epitome of hesitant obedience: he questions the truth of the angel of the LORD's words (6:13, 15, twice!), fails to recognize the angel of the LORD (6:22), asks for signs even though he knows God's will (6:17, 36–40), hesitantly tears down the village altar to Baal and Asherah (6:25) and still doesn't believe God's instruc-tions to take on the Midianites and Amalekites until God allows him to overhear a dream (7:9–15). Moreover, Gideon is the first judge in Judges to lead Israel in illegitimate worship (8:27), while his son Abimelech enters into a covenant that does not include the LORD but Baal-Berith (9:4), before he murders seventy of his brothers on one stone (9:5).

Jephthah's failure as the next judge to listen to the LORD is seen in his foolish vow (11:30) to sacrifice his daughter. It is a vow that never should have been made[6] and never should have been kept.[7] In no case should Jephthah have sacrificed his daughter as a burnt offering, for this was associated with Canaanite forms of worship and never intended by God.[8] Samson's birth is the only one in Judges that is announced by an angel with specific instruc-tions for Manoah and his wife that he live as a lifelong Nazirite and avoid: (i) touching anything ritually impure; (ii) alcohol; and (iii) cutting his hair (13:7; cf. Numbers 6:1–21). Samson, however,

---

6 The vow itself is completely unnecessary if Jephthah believed his own words to the Ammonites, which argued for the justice of the Israelite cause, before concluding that the LORD would judge the case (11:27). If he really believed in the righteousness of the Israelites' cause, then a vow attempting to "bribe" God with a sacrifice displays not only a lack of faith, but a foolish belief that a victory can be "negotiated."
7 While vows were serious business and were not to be made frivolously (Numbers 30:1–2; Deuteronomy 23:21–23), the law made provision for the redemption of vows (Leviticus 27:1–13), though not without cost.
8 "You must not worship the LORD your God in their way, because in worshiping their gods, they do all kinds of detestable things the LORD hates. They even burn their sons and daughters in the fire as sacrifices to their gods" (Deuteronomy 12:31; cf. Jeremiah 7:31:32:35). The request that Abraham sacrifice his son Isaac (Genesis 22:1–19) is a tough one, but is mitigated somewhat by the narrator's aside at the outset of the story that this is a test (Genesis 22:1).

violates these strictures (14:6–8; 16:19), not to mention other commands, like avoiding adultery (16:1; cf. Exodus 20:14; Deuteronomy 5:18).

4. Not listening—The conclusion

As we have seen, things keep getting worse the further you go in the book of Judges. The people of Israel's willingness (and ability) to listen to the voice and instructions of the LORD hits rock bottom in Judges 17–21. The story of Micah and his family (17:1–18:31) further exemplifies the pattern of failing to listen to God. Micah not only steals money from his mother, but she then turns around and not only blesses him but commissions the fabrication of an idol image and a cast idol (17:3), violating the laws against the making of idols (Exodus 20:4). Things only get worse when the tribe of Dan steals Micah's idols and perpetuates Micah's apostasy at a tribal, and later, a nation-wide level (18:30–31; cf. 1 Kings 12:29–30). The "kicker" is that Micah and his family, and even the Danites, *thought* that they were doing the right thing—they had wandered so far from God that they could no longer accurately discern what God really wanted.

The situation is even worse in Judges 19–21 when Israel begins a civil war that almost annihilates the Benjamites. This brings us back to our original starting place. It seems at first that the LORD is complicit in Israel's attempts to completely annihilate the Benjamites. But Israel's three inquiries exhibit a singular lack of ability to discern God's voice. Israel's first inquiry ("Who of us is to go up first to fight against the Benjamites?" 20:18) isn't the right question to ask—the first question to ask is "Should we go fight the Benjamites in the first place?" When God answers back that Judah should go first, Israel ignores God's voice and all Israel attacks, and so is defeated. The next day, Israel again aligns itself for battle despite their defeat (which should have been a strong clue that something was amiss) *before* inquiring of God, seemingly trying to shade the outcome of their inquiry (20:22–23). Again asking the wrong question, and getting the answer they want, they set out but are again cut down. Military defeat in the Old Testament was a strong clue that Israel was "way out of whack" in their relationship with God (Leviticus 26:17; Deuteronomy 28:25), and repeated defeat at the hands of a smaller opposing force should have caused Israel to drop to their knees and seek God in repentance, as in the days of Joshua and the first battle of Ai (Joshua 7:1–11). Yet, even Israel's double defeat only brings Israel to tears—not repentance.

Finally, on the third try, the Israelites ask the right question: "Shall we go up again to fight against the Benjamites, our fellow Israelites, *or not*?"(20:28). The LORD again answers affirmatively, but this time confirms the victory. Yet again, Israel is so far out of tune with God's will that, rather than merely extracting justice for the Benjamites crimes, they seek revenge and take things way too far, almost annihilating the Benjamites before blaming God for their excessive zeal (21:3). Israel is so insensitive to God's purposes that their solution to the dilemma they have created only creates more injustices (the complete annihilation of Israelite Jabesh Gilead [21:10–12]; and the abduction of the daughters of Shiloh as war brides [21:21]). The conclusion to the entire book, "In those days there was no king in Israel. Everyone did what was right in his own eyes" (21:25) simply punctuates the point: Israel has grown so cold to the voice of God that they can no longer accurately discern his voice or instructions. They try to push their own agenda and go to God with a pre-determined course of action. Without godly leadership focused upon hearing and meditating on the Word of God, like that advocated in Deuteronomy 17:18–19, chaos ensues. The kings of Israel were instructed to always have the law of the LORD with them, and to read it daily "that he may learn to fear the LORD his God by keeping all the words of this law and these statutes, and doing them."

5. Leadership lessons from Judges

I think there are several leadership lessons that we can take from what we see in the book of Judges:

1. Repeated and sustained reluctance to listen to God's voice can eventually result in an inability to discern the voice and direction of God as we instead "do what is right in our own eyes."

2. All leaders, even godly leaders, are susceptible to this temptation. Hebrews 11:32 includes Gideon, Barak, Jephthah and Samson among the examples of faith, and yet even these leaders were guilty of failing to really listen to God's voice. This is a powerful reminder of how careful we need to be to not let sin take root in our hearts.

3. The scary part is that in many cases in the book of Judges, Israel's leaders were not even aware of their inability to accurately discern the voice of God. Jephthah, for example, seems to be unaware of the provisions in the law for the redemption of vows. Micah thinks he is doing the right thing when he appoints his son, and then later a Levite as priests for his illegitimate backyard shrine (17:5, 9–10). Without testing their actions against the words of God, Israel and its leaders became increasingly unaware of the depths of their slide into sin. These chapters are a stark reminder of the need for all of us to guard against rationalizing our own preferences and to constantly test our words, attitudes, decisions and actions against the Word of God.

4. In the book of Judges, when the leaders of Israel fail to fully pay attention to God's instructions, this trait eventually spreads from its leaders to the people of Israel. One of the most humbling and weighty responsibilities of leadership is that when leadership fails, all of God's people suffer the consequences. God's people need leaders to lead, and lead well.

5. One of the most comforting aspects of the way God works in the book of Judges is that God accomplishes his ultimate purposes despite the flaws of his servants. Despite the judges' lack of faith (Barak, Gideon) and even their selfish desires (Samson), God uses these leaders to accomplish his intended purposes, working through (and sometimes despite) these imperfect leaders. Let all of us, as imperfect leaders, give thanks to God for his grace and his willingness to continue to use such inadequate vessels.

I echo Paul's words: "The saying is trustworthy and deserving of full acceptance, that Christ Jesus came into the world to save sinners, of whom I am the foremost. But I received mercy for this reason, that in me, as the foremost, Jesus Christ might display his perfect patience as an example to those who were to believe in him for eternal life" (1 Timothy 1:15–16).

07

The pastor as poet

BY CYRIL GUÉRETTE

f you haven't yet heard it, every pastor is a wordsmith. Not nec-
essarily a Wordsworth, but one who verily knows the Word's
worth. Ever since the founder and cornerstone of the church,
Jesus Christ, first read the prophet-poet Isaiah's words to the
congregation, declaring himself their fulfilment, and began
preaching the Good News in poetic images of seeds and birds,
lost coins and oil lamps, the vocation of biblical oration has included verbal ornamentation.

After Christ, the poet-pastor Paul's words to the Philippians
were read aloud, the hymn of the *kenosis kerygma* echoing in the
ears of the hearers the humility of a King coequal with the Father
coming in the form of a servant. Likewise, the best friend of Jesus'
penned a Revelation whose barrage of imagery continually renews

imaginations generationally, while in service of his church in Ephesus this same John produced a Gospel still unrivaled literarily. Similarly, the Lord's brother James preached potent witty aphorisms with prophetic power and wisdom that puncture hearts even to this current juncture. With both content and structure the New Testament testifies to the power of poetic proclamation.

The early church fathers continued the tradition of pastors as poets. John Chrysostom, the gold-tongued, sung praises in the capital of the Empire, capturing and converting hearts to the cause of Christ. The great Gregory of Nazianzus, overseer of the council that consolidated the Creed of Nicea-Constantinople, wrote poetic orations which defended the deity of Christ against the Arians, and assured the divinity of the Spirit would become Christian orthodoxy. Ephrem the Syrian composed poems to counteract the gains made by the heresies of Bardaisan and his son Harmonius. Furthermore, both Gregory and Ephrem's poetic constructions called out the neo-pagan Emperor Julian as he attempted to push Christianity out of Roman territory. In the West, Augustine also wrote sermons filled with poetic devices, including an entire psalmic sermon against the faction of Donatus.

A millennium later, in the evangelical English tradition, John Bunyan stands out as a pastor whose poetic sensibility helped shape our entire language, while Andrew Fuller's own penchant for verse was an invaluable voice amongst the Baptists. Charles and John Wesley, Isaac Watts, John Newton and numerous others, all demonstrate that when a pastor puts his heart and mind to the poetic aspect of the calling, the results can be quite inspiring.

Yet, it is not simply history that attests to the poet as pastor, it is also the poetics of homiletics itself that requires every pastor pay attention to the aesthetic dimension. As Spurgeon called the pastor to give due diligence to the human voice, we observe an understanding of the relationship between poetry and the homily. In Greek, the term *poesis* itself refers to a creating, a making, and reminds us that it is easy to forget that in crafting any sermon, poetry is present. The linguist Roman Jakobson refers to the poetic element of language as a focus on the message itself, a fusion of form and function. Surely every pastor should thus respect the poetic as part and parcel of preaching. How the message is constructed can sometimes be as important as what is being said.

Augustine hoped to train young future pastors in *On Christian Teaching*, dedicating sections to both the interpretation of Scripture and the formation of orations. He pointed out that in God is found both *Truth* and *Beauty*. If a pastor were to preach a sermon that was truthful in every detail, but had no beauty whatsoever, it would be boring, and cause many in the audience to miss out on the truth within completely. He himself had ignored the Christian faith for years because he considered its language unrefined, a misconception the poetic sermons of Ambrose helped dispel. On the other hand, if a sermon was the most beautiful in form and pleasant to the ear beyond compare, but taught falsehood, it would be worthless or worse yet, like a delicious meal that was full of poison. It is because of the danger of the potential pull of poetic fictitious lies that Augustine ultimately privileges the truth aspect of language over beauty, saying a good intellect doesn't love words but the truth in words. Still, if a sentence is written with a profound truth but expressed without clarity (an element of beauty) then it can also be dangerous and accidently misleading. Truth and beauty are inextricably intertwined, and the goal of the preacher is to have both right instruction and delight coalesce in our words and reinforce each other so that both the truth and the beauty of God are experienced in unity and draw the audience closer to him.

If the idea of pastors concerning themselves more consciously with beauty seems foreign, it must be remembered that the beauty of the Lord is a theme explored over and over in the Bible. The Psalms especially both discuss and display this aesthetic theme powerfully. The psalmist declares in Psalm 27:4, "One thing I ask from the Lord, this only do I seek: that I may dwell in the house of the Lord all the days of my life, to gaze on the beauty of the Lord and to seek him in his temple." The truth of God is evident throughout the Psalms, with many of the major attributes of God and propositions concerning created reality being clearly stated. At the same time, this propositional truth is clothed in the poetic forms of parallelism, simile, metaphor, merism, inclusio, chiasmus, acrostic, metonymy, synecdoche, apostrophe, wordplays and many others, perhaps even including rhyme.

The prophets likewise found that one of the most effective ways to both communicate the truth of God and produce the right emotional reaction to the word, was to utilize poetic devices and forms that engaged and sometimes even enraged the audience. The pastor must remember their affectivity as both priest and prophet increases as they embrace the reality that they are poets.

The preaching pastor is a poet simply by way of his oral proclamation. Reclamation of this reality can only assist in producing more effective vocal communication. For a sermon is not simply informative, but performative. The way the words sound can make more profound what we expound. This is grounded in the way in which God created humanity. From infancy, before comprehending a whit of a word, a child may giggle in sheer joy at a well-crafted rhyming sentence. It is this musicality of words, the tonality of utterance, with which God has gifted his people. And one may maintain that music is a mystery, which only God could explain. Pain and joy, fear and loathing, celebration and consolation, are all contained within the notes of the octave. Musicologists and aestheticians debate how exactly our emotions are evoked so provocatively through patterned sounds, but the phenomenological reality is undeniable. That words can map onto these musical notations and rhythms is the key to why truth and beauty in a pastor's speech is so important to recognize. The power of Martin Luther King Jr.'s refrain of "I have a dream" comes from matching the truth of his prophetic message with the beauty of his baritone intonations.

This musicality of words is an important piece of every preacher's repertoire, and something honed through practice, if not intentionality. The more conscious we become of its power, the more useful it becomes at our disposal. Thus it is my proposal that every pastor embrace their inner poet.

Practically, the reality of the pastor as poet will be worked out in each pulpit, with the insight, sensitivity, and distinctive gifting of the individual creating a unique poetic voice as it exposits Holy Writ.

That being said, it may be of some use to offer some insights gained from poetically self-conscious study and practice for those awakening to the poetic reality of their vocation. In that light, I would propose a few ways in which the idea of pastor as poet may become instantiated in the regular exposition of Scripture in the service of the church.

A simple way to begin exploring the poetic dimension of homiletics is to begin better utilizing already existent poems in the body of one's sermon. The psalms, prophets and poetic parts of narratives and epistles of Scripture are obviously great material in such usage. It is important to unleash the poetic quality of these passages as you deliver them orally, tapping into the ancient power of poetry that the Spirit of God providentially embedded within them. One should practice reading such passages beforehand, speaking them slowly and powerfully, expressing the emotion with which the heart of God wrote them. Each line should be given attention, including how it relates to both the preceding lines and those succeeding. Raise your voice when the text demands it, and rush into a holy hush when it complements best. A great way to practice is to read through the psalms and prophets out loud to oneself in times of devotional study, as it will at the same time impregnate your own use of language with the linguistic rhythms that can only increase the poetic and emotional power of your original sermon compositions.

Building upon this, it is useful to begin to familiarize yourself with extra-biblical English poetry, especially Christian greats such as Milton, Herbert, Donne, Coleridge, Wordsworth, Hopkins and Eliot. Likewise spend time reading to yourself the magnificent hymns of Watts, Wesley and Fanny Crosby. There is a unique appreciation for form and content that comes from reading these hymns as opposed to singing them. A great way to spice up one's sermons, and to help acclimatize the pastor to eventually creating his own poetry, is to pepper quotations from these poets, and other classics, into the body of his homily.

For development of more modern poetic sensibilities, I'd suggest listening to and reading the lyrics to modern Christian music, including the genre of Christian Rap or Holy Hip-hop. Likewise, there is a growing body of Christian spoken word readily available online (eg. Passion 4 Christ Movement). It can be argued that the sermon is a form of spoken word, even if it must, for sake of clarity, tone down the use of poetic devices comparatively. Whatever one's age, ethnicity or culture, familiarizing oneself with these new popular expressions will form your own poetic sensibility and help reduce the probability of cheesy and corny uses of poetry in one's sermonizing and services. Quoting these artists, or incorporating their work into the service from time to time, is an effective way of allowing the power of the musicality and profundity of creative language to minister among the congregation.

If the previous recommendations are about immersing oneself in poetry, and utilizing others' work, it is important to remember that you are a poet when crafting your own sermons. Most homiletics textbooks will at least pay lip service to this reality in their advice regarding structuring a sermon, and especially when it comes to the use of illustrations. The power of stories, or analogies, in homiletics is undeniable, and pastors worth their salt know the necessity of engaging the audience with such devices. The example of Jesus' use of parables further encourages every pastor to take seriously the use of illustrative material. Pastors become proficient at looking at every event in their day for sermon potential, often not recognizing that in doing so they are proving themselves to be poets. Embracing the reality of the pastor as poet will go a long way in freeing oneself to spend even more time developing and exploring this element of the sermon, not simply because it echoes a truth stated early in propositional format, but because it often better communicates the truth than a simple argumentative sentence ever could—hence why Jesus found stories one of the most important modes for his sermonizing, often giving only minimal or even no propositional follow-up.

Moving from this area in which most pastors are comfortable with the use of a poetic device, it is important to understand that many other poetic techniques are at the disposal of the pastor. Repetition is one that is quickly recognizable; it is common practice to repeat a key phrase, or the same main point in different words, to be sure that the homiletic purpose of the individual sermon is fulfilled. Think again of Martin Luther King's continued repetition of the refrain, "I have a dream." This famous repetition did not cause boredom in the audience, but the exact opposite, it evoked the emotions in an unforgettable manner.

This principle can be further applied to the effectiveness of the repetition of sounds. Other very useful related poetic devices in the modern sermon come from forms of sound repetition, especially alliteration (the repetition of the first letter or letters of words) and rhyme (the repetition of the sound of a syllable). A little alliteration allows all the literate in the congregation to alter their attention and attitude in appreciation to the Almighty's appropriation.

Now this is where many readers may begin to become a bit squeamish. It's one thing to read Scripture more dramatically, quote poems and hone sermon illustrations; it's another altogether to deliver timely rhyme and alliteration. This is true, and important to recognize. Firstly, if one has too much adoration for verbal ornamentation, it can quickly distract from the point of the sermon itself. If the audience is paying too much attention to the way the message is spoken, they might miss what is spoken. This is why the ancient teachers of rhetoric made clarity one of the most important qualities to incorporate into speech. Especially if one is dealing with a complicated bit of exegesis in a difficult passage, the last thing needed is to have jarring sentence structure affect the ability to concentrate. Secondly, if one delivers rhyme and alliteration in a manner too self-conscious it can affect their potential power to seal the doctrinal point home in the mind of the audience with a proper emotion that attends.

For these reasons, it is recommended that one does not draw attention to the fact that alliteration or rhyme are being used, their impact will be subconsciously just as powerful whether or not the audience is cognizant of the devices. For smoother delivery, it might be useful to fully write out the text manuscript in places where more poetic language is planned.

Short curt sentences are best;
Set out simply from the rest.

This allows you to read from the script easily, and deliver the lines more effectively.

The point is to be conscious of the sound of the sermon, to pay attention to the oral dimension. Aristotle advises that highly emotional speech and poetic devices are best saved for conclusions, once the facts have been delivered, to bolster your argument. Thus, purposefully poetic elements can be useful at the end of major sermon sections, or even to summarize a powerful point in the middle of a section. The final conclusion of the sermon is one of the most important places to employ poetic devices. When one is helping the audience see how to respond to the truth teased out of a biblical passage, alliteration and rhyme can chime in subtly to support. Poetic language swoops in with the inherent power of the musicality of words, coupling the proper emotional response to the propositional content. The pastoral heart is serving by observing the oral arts.

This is the unity of verity and beauty in theology.

With the psalmist the pastor can sing:

My heart is stirred by a noble theme
    as I recite my verses for the king;
    my tongue is the pen of a skillful writer. [Psalm 45:1]

Every pastor is a poet; it's about time we/they know it.

08

Singles in the church

BY MARIANNE VANDERBOOM

When I was twenty and starting my adult life, I never imagined the direction it would take. I assumed, as I suspect most people do, that I would get married and have a family, grow old with my spouse and die surrounded by children and grandchildren. I didn't consciously decide I wanted or didn't want this. To be honest, I didn't know there was any other option. I believed it was my duty; it was what was expected. I never heard there could be another way. It didn't occur to me that God might have another plan for my life.

But he did have a different plan. I never got married. I never had children. Instead, my life has been full of crazy opportunities to serve him in ways I could never do if I had followed the traditional trajectory. It has been a rich and wonderful adventure. And he has a different plan for so many. There are the ones, like me, who never got married. There are the ones who married and had a family only to find him or herself widowed. Or divorced. We sit in church alone. We are single. And we are a growing segment of the church body.

As it did when I was growing up, however, it still often feels that the single state is not a legitimate option. If singleness is acknowledged to be an option, it is inferior to that of marriage. Although that is rarely said outright in churches, the implicit curriculum (that which we do) and the null curriculum (the things we never talk about or never do) can lead singles to believe they are sub-members, that God can't really use singles, and that singleness is a flaw that needs to be fixed.

Perhaps that's what the body of Christ really believes. Perhaps my brothers and sisters in Christ really do look on me with pity, viewing me as incomplete and insufficient without a spouse by my side. Perhaps the church really does believe that being single is a sad second-best. However, I'd like to think better of my brothers and sisters. I'd like to believe that the message I receive is unintentional, and caused by a lack of awareness rather than by any kind of deliberate rejection. So I have compiled a list of ways a church can change the message and remove the stigma we face because of our singleness.

This list is not comprehensive, nor will it resonate with every single person or every church. It is merely a starting point, a way to begin the conversation with the singles in our congregations.

1. Preach about the blessings of being single.

I have listened to many sermons that are addressed specifically to those who are married and who have families. I celebrate marriage, I really do. I understand that it is a God-given and sacred state. But so is singleness, and I have never heard a single sermon preached on it. Preach about the blessings of being single. Paul did (2 Corinthians 7). The best that might happen is to add a few lines to a sermon on marriage in a valiant attempt to make it somehow applicable to singles. But being single comes with unique blessings and opportunities which deserve to be celebrated and embraced by the worshipping community. Don't stop preaching about marriage—just start preaching also about singleness and how it is an equally valid sacred state. Present it as a legitimate and God-honouring option.

2. When you encourage congregational involvement in a sermon, be inclusive.

Do not ask your congregation, "Turn to the person you came with and say...." I didn't come with anyone. I'm not sitting with anyone. I might be sitting *beside* people, but I'm not sitting *with* them. When I am asked to turn to the person sitting with me, I feel excluded. When someone is single again, it is a painful and unnecessary reminder of the change of his/her marital status. It is safe to assume that there are lots of people in our churches who came alone.

3. Allow us to spend time with the families and couples in the church.

While there are times when I might want to hang out with other singles, there are also lots of times when I would love to be around families, to hang out with men and women my own age, to play with kids, to just be part of a family without feeling obliged to be the babysitter while the adults hang out together. Those who have been widowed or divorced already have connections with families and couples. It is cruel to sever them from their support network because of a change in their marital status, and it serves to reinforce the message that the unmarried are only half-people. Ministry to singles and singles-again cannot consist of simply isolating them into homogeneous groups; it must involve incorporating them fully into the body of Christ.

4. When you are offering a special event at your church, have equally priced ticketing.

When I see tickets offered for sale, "$10/single or $15/couple," I feel punished for my singleness. What's worse is that I don't even feel like I can bring a girlfriend and qualify for the "couple" price, because we are not a couple. Why not just make all the tickets the same price? Tickets sold at women-only or men-only events are rarely sold "two-for-the-price-of-one." So why do it for mixed-gender events? And while you're at it, when you're setting up tables, especially round tables, set a few of them with seven places instead of eight. Not everyone is coming in pairs.

5. Trust us.

This one is a bit hard to define, but it boils down to a sense that singles are somehow a threat or hindrance to healthy marriages. A person I know, fairly new to a church, signed up for a small group. She was contacted by the leader of a group and accepted into the group. But when the group leader found out that the woman was single, the woman was informed she couldn't be in the group after all. Why not? Does having one single or one single-again or one widow(er) in the group so throw off the dynamics of that group that the single just can't be there? Does being single trump my humanness? Does it mean that I don't have an adult understanding of adult issues? Are you afraid that our presence is going to break up marriages? Trust us. We don't want your husband or wife. We are human beings with experiences that range far beyond our singleness. We are perfectly capable of holding our own in adult conversation. We might even have something to contribute. There is no need to keep us away from the married people in the church.

6. Respect our time.

There have been many occasions where people have made the assumption that I spend hours alone at home sitting by the phone waiting for a phone call and can make plans at the drop of a hat, or that I have long hours of free time to spend doing the volunteer tasks in the church that need doing. People have said to me, "Well, you don't have a family, so you have the time to do this." By all means, ask, but don't presume I have time. And I'd love to visit, but advance notice is nice. Being single gives me lots of time to be busy!

7. Don't treat us as a problem to be solved.

I'm trying to keep this list positive, to give ideas that *can* be done rather than a list of things that shouldn't be done, but this next one just can't be worded positively: Don't treat us as a problem to be solved. I have been at the receiving end of all of these words: "How come a nice girl like you is still single?" "What's wrong with you, that you're still single?" "But you *want* to get married, right?" "Are you a feminist?" "You must be so lonely." "You must be too picky." I have had well-meaning people try to set me up. I had a lady once invite me to her place for Christmas dinner, with the words, "My husband and I are giving up our own Christmas to invite all the single people who have nowhere else to go." I've had people assume I live a narrow little life where the only meaningful thing I have is my work. I live a rich and fulfilling life, full of exciting opportunities to serve God which would not have been open to me if I had gotten married and had a family. Sure, there are times when I am lonely; so are many of the married people I know. Sure, things are not always perfect or ideal; name a life where they are. There is nothing wrong with me. I am not looking to change my marital state. My singleness is not a problem, and even if it was, I would not be looking for judgement or pity. I'd much rather you get to know me as an individual instead of seeing me as a problem that needs to be solved.

8. Being single does present unique challenges.
All of that being said, being single does present unique challenges. Issues like illness and unemployment take on a greater weight when you live alone and are your sole breadwinner. Extended community becomes of greater importance if we are to avoid becoming isolated. Learning to live in purity in a sexually charged world takes on different nuances. Allow us to express those challenges without thinking (or worse, saying) that marriage will solve them all. I cannot think of any significant problem I have faced as a single that married people haven't also struggled with in some form or another. Marriage is not the solution to my problems; Jesus is. Be willing to help singles to deal with those challenges without pressuring us to change our marital state. Getting married won't fix our challenges. It will just replace them with new challenges that might be more familiar to you, and thus, more in your comfort zone. Be willing to learn. Be willing to listen. Be willing to explore, as the body of Christ, both the joys and the challenges of being a follower of Jesus who is single, and to work together to celebrate and meet those joys and challenges in Christ.

Congregations are made of a mix of people, young and old, married and single, and single-again. Get to know us singles. We have gifts and talents which are needed to build up the body of Christ. We are pretty normal people, with fears and hopes, dreams and broken dreams, heartaches and joys, challenges and blessings, just like any other member of the congregation. Encourage us and allow us to get involved in ways that fully use our gifts. Where we lack immediate family, be the family of Christ. Accept that singles have a valuable role to play in the body of Christ. Celebrate singleness in the way that Paul does. The body of Christ will only be strengthened. Singleness should be accepted as the God-honouring, sacred state that the apostle Paul believed it is. As the church of Christ, we can speak and act in ways that shows we believe this to be true, and remove the stigma of being single.

09

Rethinking Christian funerals

BY STAN FOWLER

don't suppose I ever enjoyed going to funerals, but I often find them unbearable now. I was a university student before I attended my first funeral, and I think I had been to only two or three before I became a pastor. When I was only about three months into my first pastoral ministry, the church treasurer died of a sudden heart attack, and suddenly I was thinking about funerals. I've thought a lot about them over the years, and I've seen many changes, some for the better and some, I think, for the worse. There are plenty of reasons to dislike funerals, of course, not the least of which is the general discomfort most of us feel when dealing with death. I'm sure I'm not alone in feeling some dislike for funerals.

I am, however, thinking of a much more important reason for disliking most of the funerals I have attended in the last few years, most of which were evangelical Christian funerals. What I have in mind is the depressing lack of biblical content in the services and what seems to be the misplaced focus. Christian hope as found in Scripture is focused on our future resurrection at the return of Christ and our eternal life as whole persons, body and soul, in a redeemed universe. However, in many Christian funerals, there is no mention at all of our future resurrection rooted in the resurrection of our Lord. The idea of resurrection seems to be a well kept secret.

This observation has, I confess, made me a funeral critic, so that I listen very closely to the expression of hope in the service, sometimes counting the references to resurrection. That is not a burdensome task, given the general lack of such references. As I write this, I am thinking back to the funerals that I have attended in the last few years. Some of the deceased were members of my church, some were pastors whom I have known and some were Christian leaders with national influence. The tributes given by family members and friends were well deserved in every case. It was appropriate to remember the positive influence of these people on many others. But the expression of Christian hope in many of these services never went beyond the affirmation that those who had died were now in the presence of the Lord. To make matters worse, some of the speakers referred to what was supposedly happening now in heaven in speculative terms far beyond anything revealed in Scripture. I don't doubt that the deceased believers are with the Lord, but the impression given was that they had entered into their final experience of salvation when they died and went to heaven. That just doesn't match the biblical view of salvation.

Let me be clear, I am not denying that those who believe in Christ enter into his presence in a disembodied state at death. The apostle Paul viewed death as the door to being with Christ, a condition better than that of this life (Philippians 1), and he spoke of post-mortem existence as "absent from the body and present with the Lord" (2 Corinthians 5:8). There is also Jesus' description of the rich man and the beggar Lazarus in Luke 16, although it is not clear how literally the story is to be read, given its description of bodily parts in the life after death. Do believers enter the presence of Christ at death? Yes. Is that the fulfillment of Christian hope rooted in Christ's victory over death? No. It is just the first step beyond this life, an interim existence in which we wait for resurrection and final judgement at the return of our Lord in glory. As N.T. Wright has stated so well in his book, *Surprised by Hope*,[1] what we look for is "the life after life after death." God created humans to live as embodied creatures, and as long as our bodies are lying in the grave, death is an enemy not yet fully defeated. We were not created to live as disembodied souls, and God's purpose in redemption includes the ultimate reversal of death.

This perspective is really very clear in the New Testament. There is, in fact, a biblical text addressed to Christians telling them how to think about hope when confronted by the death of Christian loved ones, namely, 1 Thessalonians 4:13–18. Paul asserts that just as God raised Jesus from the dead, so also he will bring those who belong to Jesus into the same experience (v. 14). That will happen at the return of Christ, when "the dead in Christ will rise first" (v. 16). Paul says nothing at all in that text about what happens at death—instead the whole focus of the text is on what will happen at our future resurrection. The same sort of emphasis is found in 1 Corinthians 15 where the entire chapter is devoted to an emphatic affirmation of the bodily resurrection of the dead, prefigured and promised by the resurrection of Christ, "the firstfruits" (v. 20). The victory of Christ will not be complete until he has evacuated the graves and displayed his conquest of death itself (v. 26).

The texts in 1 Thessalonians 4 and 1 Corinthians 15 are the most fully developed statements of the centrality of future resurrection in Christian eschatology, but there are other allusions as well. In Romans 8, Paul refers to the present suffering of both humans and the creation in which we live, and he asserts that God's redemptive work includes the liberation of the creation from its bondage to decay (v. 21). Our bodies are part of that created order, and Paul teaches us that the salvation for which we wait in hope (vv. 24–25) includes the "redemption of our bodies" (v. 23). This is not a spiritualized redemption *from* our bodies as disembodied souls, but the redemption *of* our bodies. In his letter

---

1 N.T. Wright, *Surprised by Hope: Rethinking Heaven, the Resurrection, and the Mission of the Church* (New York: HarperOne, 2008).

to the Philippians, Paul reminds his readers that we are waiting for our Saviour to return from heaven, when he will transform our humble bodies into "the likeness of his glorious body" (Philippians 3:20–21). The final biblical description of our hope is seen in Revelation 21–22, and the picture there is one of a redeemed cosmos inhabited by the resurrected saints. It is not a picture of souls being liberated from bodies and going to heaven, but a picture of a new heaven *and a new earth*, and *God comes down* to dwell with his people. We weren't made to live as disembodied souls in heaven, but to live as embodied persons serving as stewards of God's good creation, and in the end that is what we will be. In spite of the common rhetoric, the Bible does not describe final salvation as "going to heaven," and no continual use of the words will make it so.

It may be helpful to stop and think about the terminology that we commonly use to talk about the death of our family and friends. In my circles, it seems that what I regularly hear is that someone "passed away," which has been common terminology for as long as I can remember. But now I frequently hear the noun form, "passing" as a way of describing someone's death. I would not want to say that description of death as "passing" is inaccurate or wrong, but I wonder sometimes if the euphemism is rooted in an inappropriate discomfort with the word "death." Now I realize that the apostle Paul uses the euphemism of "sleep" sometimes to describe the death of believers (in both 1 Thessalonians 4 and 1 Corinthians 15), and for that reason it would be wrong to say that we must always use the term "die," but I still wonder if we have lost some awareness of the dark side of death.

Another piece of evangelical jargon about death is to say that "the Lord took her home" or to describe the death as "her homegoing." Perhaps this a good way to say it, because our life is in Christ, and in some way home is wherever he is, and Paul makes it clear that our citizenship is in heaven (Philippians 3:20). But I wonder: God did not make us to live in heaven—he made us to live as his image here on earth, functioning as his vice-regents in our rule over the created order. To say that our citizenship is in heaven is not to say that our home is in heaven, only that our ultimate allegiance is to God in heaven. Peter does refer to our inheritance that is reserved in heaven (1 Peter 1:4), but this is a "salvation ready to be revealed in the last time" (v. 5) when Jesus Christ is revealed (v. 8), that is, at his glorious return to earth to judge and reign. While it might be right to speak of our death as our homegoing in one sense, it would be wrong to mean by the term that we were made for heaven *as opposed to earth*. Therefore, I would suggest that we might better say, "The Lord took her to himself," rather than, "The Lord took her home."

What, then, should we call the public gatherings at which we mark the death of our friends? I have used the term "funeral" here in this article, but that does not seem to be the common term these days. The term "memorial service" is much more common in my circles, and it is appropriate in many ways. However, the term focuses on remembering the past, and while that is one reason that we gather, surely as believers in Christ we ought also to look forward and remind one another of the hope of final salvation yet to come. The other term that has become quite common is "celebration of life." In some ways this is simply saying the same thing as "memorial service," but it says it more emphatically. It is fitting, of course, to give thanks for the positive impact of the person's life and to celebrate the grace of God that made it a reality, but my sense is that the term is designed to do more than that. I get the impression that this description of the event is often designed to deny that we are gathering to grieve in any significant way, and if so, then the term is problematic. As Paul puts it in 1 Corinthians 15, death is a result of Adam's fall and a continuing enemy, a foe to be defeated by resurrection. I am not arguing here that all alternatives to "funeral" are terms that must be rejected; my point is that whatever terms we use, we need to remember to do more at the death of a Christian than to remember the good things about their life that is past. We also need to grieve the end of that good life and to affirm that the presence of the body in the grave is not the last word.

Scripture exhorts us to "teach one another in psalms, hymns, and spiritual songs" (Colossians 3:16), and it is surely true that much of what we believe is what we have learned from the songs that we sing. What can be said, then, about the songs concerning the life to come? Or the songs about the resurrection of Jesus and its implications? The news, I suggest, is not so good, and I give one example, a song explicitly intended to show the connection between the resurrection of Jesus and our hope. I refer to the well-known song, "Because He Lives," written by Bill and Gloria Gaither, sung around the world for decades and often at Christian funerals. The refrain locates our hope for the future in Jesus' resurrection:

> Because he lives, I can face tomorrow.
> Because he lives, all fear is gone.
> Because I know he holds the future,
> And life is worth the living, just because he lives.

The third and final stanza expresses this hope for the future:

> And then one day, I'll cross the river.
> I'll fight life's final war with pain,
> And then as death gives way to victory,
> I'll see the lights of glory, and I'll know he reigns.

Thus, the ultimate statement of hope in the song is our experience at death, and that is phrased in terms of victory, a term that Paul reserves for the granting of immortality at bodily resurrection (1 Corinthians 15:50–57). Although the song expresses Christian truth, it never gets to the main point. It lacks the final stanza that would joyfully affirm the biblical connection between the resurrection of Jesus and our future resurrection at his return. The resurrection of Jesus is the paradigm, because he is the "firstborn from among the dead" (Colossians 1:18) and the "firstfruits" (1 Corinthians 15:20). Jesus' victory over death did not occur when he died—it was on the third day—and our victory over death will be complete only when our Lord returns to empty the graves. Perhaps I should try to get Bill and Gloria to write that stanza.

My appeal to pastors and others involved in planning Christian funerals is to think carefully and biblically about the nature of our hope as believers in the risen Lord. There are many appropriate components in a genuinely Christian funeral: expressions of grief; biblical texts that speak of God's comforting presence; prayers asking for comfort; eulogies that give thanks for the work of grace in the deceased; biblical texts that declare the good news of Jesus' death and resurrection; prayers that affirm the gospel; biblical texts that declare our hope of resurrection; songs that declare our hope in Christ; and preaching that orients us to the basis and nature of our hope. What is so often said at Christian funerals is not false as much as it is incomplete. The fuller picture conveyed in Scripture does not deny that deceased Christians are with the Lord, but it does expand our hope to affirm confidently "the sure and certain hope of the resurrection of the dead." Being absent from the body and present with the Lord is good, but as good as that is, there is something far better that lies ahead when Christ comes again to make all things new. That's worth saying at Christian funerals.[2]

---

2 The seminary professor who revolutionized my appreciation for the possibilities of biblical preaching, Haddon Robinson, once quipped, "Sacred cows make the best hamburger, but sometimes the meat is hard to swallow." I've played the butcher in some ways here, and I understand that it may not go down easily, but I'm not the first to make these points, and if you want to pursue this in more detail. here are some places to start. I referred already to N.T. Wright's book, *Surprised by Hope*, which explores questions about resurrection and the nature of eternal life in great detail. I don't agree with everything in the book, but it is clearly worth reading. Tom Wright is always stimulating, but I confess that he annoys me with his tendency to write as if he is the first person to get these things right. He shows little awareness that the Dutch Reformed tradition has had a strong grasp of the biblical focus on resurrection and the redemption of the cosmos. One very helpful statement from that tradition can be found in Anthony Hoekema, *The Bible and the Future* (Grand Rapids: Eerdmans, 1979). Some of the best work in recent years has been done by Michael Wittmer (a theologian at Grand Rapids Theological Seminary) in his books *Heaven Is a Place on Earth* (Grand Rapids: Zondervan, 2004) and *The Last Enemy: Preparing to Win the Fight of Your Life* (Grand Rapids: Discovery House, 2012). Mike writes in a lively and engaging way, and his books will stimulate both your mind and your heart, not to mention strengthening your hope rooted in the work of our resurrected Lord.

Afterword

FROM HERITAGE COLLEGE & SEMINARY

"What makes your school effective?" This is the question that prompted this little book project. We answer the question by seeking to be valuable to the church. "Scholars in service of the church." So now we ask the question, "Who and what is Heritage, and how does it fulfil that goal?"

Heritage College & Seminary in Cambridge, Ontario, Canada, is the product of the merging of its two founding schools in 1993, London Baptist Bible College and Seminary (London, Ontario) and Central Baptist Seminary (Toronto, Ontario). The vision of these schools has always been to train pastors, missionaries and workers for the church. This is captured in our institutional mission statement which reads:

Heritage College & Seminary exists to glorify God by partnering with churches in providing a biblically-based education equipping people for life and ministry in the church and world.

Heritage College is an undergraduate school offering BTh, BRE, and BCM degrees with majors and minors in pastoral studies, missions, children and family ministry, music and worship, youth ministry and more. The college also has a one-year certificate entitled, "eQuip" which is designed for students who wish to spend a year at a Bible college after high school before they move on to further education or enter the workforce.

Heritage Seminary is a graduate school offering Master of Divinity (MDiv) and Master of Theological Studies (MTS) degrees. The MDiv degree has tracks in pastoral studies, missions and a general track. An undergraduate degree is required to enter one of these masters programs. The seminary also offers diplomas and certificates in biblical studies and pastoral ministry for students without undergraduate degrees.

As a college and seminary, we hold to the conviction that God has revealed himself through creation and the written Word. We believe that the Bible in its original autographs is verbally inspired of God, inerrant and the final authority in what we believe and how we live. As a result of this belief, we base our education in the Word of God, seek to apply its principles in all areas of life, and see it as the integrating factor for all of life.

Ministering to the whole person is important to us. Our faculty are serious and competent scholars and academics. We work hard at providing a quality educational experience through a good library and thoughtful teaching. However, all our faculty have sincere pastoral hearts, and the Bible college and seminary experience goes way beyond mere information, both inside and outside the classroom. Being a smaller school, we get to know our students well, and there is a strong emphasis on spiritual formation for every student, as well as for faculty, staff and administration. Institutional chapels play a significant role in Heritage life, and various conferences (eg. missions conference, spiritual life conference) and seminar days (eg. Ministry Leadership Day) contribute to the holistic experience of Heritage students. College students can enjoy an active and integrative community life through the residences, and connection with the college and its student life brings added benefits to the seminary community.

We've articulated the following goals for Heritage graduates:

Spiritual: Demonstrates a growing personal relationship with God that is evidenced through consistent Christian conduct.

Physical: Practices a healthy lifestyle.

Social: Exhibits cultural awareness and appropriate skills in personal relationships.

Intellectual: Thinks critically, is competent in biblical, general and professional studies, and is maturing in Bible-based convictions.

Emotional: Understands the nature of emotions and expresses them appropriately.

Cultural: Has acquired an increased understanding of global ideas and events, and has developed an international mind-set, and is prepared to live and speak redemptively in the world.

Professional: Has developed skills as a vocational or non-vocational servant for the church of Jesus Christ according to aptitudes, gifts, and abilities.

Aesthetic: Has an appreciation for and participates in wholesome expressions of culture.

Our vision is that we would see Heritage College & Seminary become a leader in local and global church leadership and ministry, and that we would do that through biblical and competent teaching, helpful structures and administration, relevant curricula, diverse and flexible delivery systems, a Great Commission orientation and a holistic spiritual and ministry formation experience. As such, we see ourselves strategically placed in the evangelical context to serve a significant number of churches, denominations and Christian ministries.

We are accredited with the Association of Higher Biblical Education (ABHE), and at present have associate status with the Association of Theological Schools (ATS). We are presently working on moving to candidate and full status in the next couple of years with ATS.

Heritage's influence extends globally with over 2,500 alumni around the world. By God's grace we seek to be effective in our value to the church, and to see our influence continue to grow, and to continue to serve the cause of Christ, his church and his mission in the world for many years to come. *To him be the glory.*

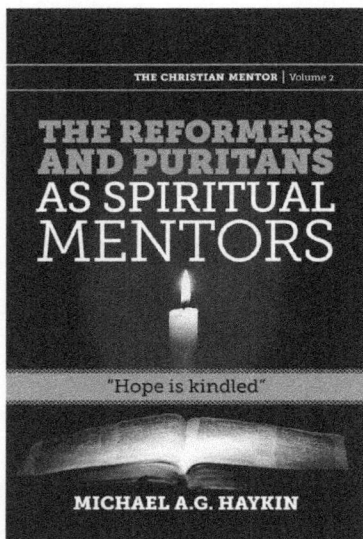

The Christian Mentor | Volume 2

The reformers and Puritans as spiritual mentors
"Hope is kindled"

By Michael A.G. Haykin

REFORMERS SUCH as Tyndale, Cranmer and Calvin, and Puritans Richard Greenham, John Owen, etc. are examined to see how their display of the light of the gospel provides us with models of Christian conviction and living.

ISBN 978–1–894400–39–8

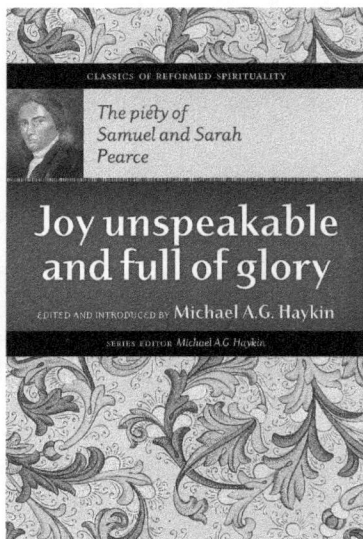

Classics of Reformed spirituality

Joy unspeakable and full of glory
The piety of Samuel and Sarah Pearce

By Michael A.G. Haykin

SAMUEL PEARCE played a key role in the formation and early days of the Baptist Missionary Society in eighteenth-century England. Through Samuel and Sarah's letters we are given a window into their rich spiritual life and living piety.

ISBN 978–1–894400–48–0

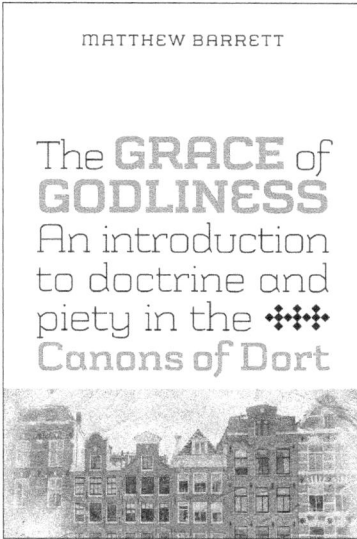

The grace of godliness

An introduction to doctrine and piety in the Canons of Dort

By Matthew Barrett

BARRETT opens a window on the synod's deliberations with the Remonstrants and examines the main emphases of the canons, with special attention on their relationship to biblical piety and spirituality.

ISBN 978-1-894400-52-7 (PB)

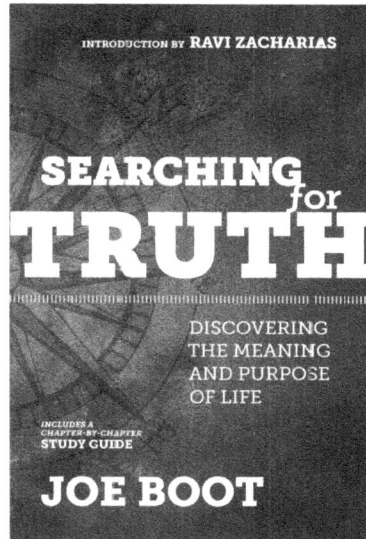

Searching for truth

Discovering the meaning and purpose of life

By Joe Boot

BEGINNING WITH a basic understanding of the world, Joe Boot explains the biblical worldview, giving special attention to the life and claims of Jesus Christ. He wrestles with questions about suffering, truth, morality and guilt.

ISBN 978-1-894400-40-4

Deo Optimo et Maximo Gloria
To God, best and greatest, be glory

joshua
p r e s s

www.joshuapress.com

www.ingramcontent.com/pod-product-compliance
Lightning Source LLC
Chambersburg PA
CBHW021937040426
42448CB00008B/1109